Endorsements for *No Less than Genius*

Dr. Mozia has written what amounts to a must read primer for anyone in the field of education, especially those interested in urban educational issues, as well as the students who are enthralled in the struggle to find some purpose in what goes on in school as they relate to life in general. This book does a great job of creating a sense of urgency and focus, while serving as a powerful call to action on how educators and non-educators alike can help instill in the youth they work with a sense of purpose relative to everything they do in school. Not only do the chapters in this book speak to the reader, they also embrace and feature all of the critical and essential concepts that could be found in any anthology in the field of education. As an urban education practitioner, administrator, and former adjunct professor of Education, I consider this book a delightful and serious guide, full of important and much needed concepts and information for both students and those educators on the front lines in all institutions charged with providing intellectual training to the youth.

~Harry Obiako, Ph.D., MBA - urban school administrator and former School of Education Adjunct Faculty

Helen Mozia's *"No Less than Genius"* is inspired by one of the most potent truisms of life: "the pull to become," which speaks to the innermost being of a child. How powerfully she demonstrates that by empowering children to discover, evolve, and deliver their unique gifts in the world, we fulfill the utmost purpose of education. May this book find its way into the hands and hearts of educators and parents who are committed to revolutionizing our educational system into one that educates from the inside out. Read this book, and then share it with all those you love.

~Michael Bernard Beckwith - author of Life Visioning

Dr. Mozia is a brilliant, inspired educator that truly has a heart for all children. This book will not only shape lives, it will help remake lives.

—Akuyoe Graham - actress and founder of
Spirit Awakening Foundation

No Less than Genius: engage, motivate and accelerate success for every youth takes learners and young adults on a journey of self-discovery and empowerment as they navigate the world of education and career.

—Mary Manin Morrissey - best-selling author, world-
renowned life coach, and motivational speaker

... a guide book every youth, especially those in high school, college, and anyone seeking a career pathway must read. *"No Less than Genius"* is strewn together with interesting and riveting anecdotes, and provides guidance to discovering one's "pull to become" and actualizing the pull. It is brilliant!

—Fola Adisa – national board certified teacher of
mathematics, Atlanta, Georgia, U.S.A.

*Engage, Motivate, and Accelerate Success for
Every Youth with the Pull to Become ...*

No Less Than
GENIUS

Dr. Helen Mozia

BALBOA.
PRESS

A DIVISION OF HAY HOUSE

Balboa Press books may be ordered through booksellers or by contacting:

Balboa Press
A Division of Hay House
1663 Liberty Drive
Bloomington, IN 47403
www.balboapress.com
1 (877) 407-4847

Because of the dynamic nature of the Internet, any web addresses or links contained in this book may have changed since publication and may no longer be valid. The views expressed in this work are solely those of the author and do not necessarily reflect the views of the publisher, and the publisher hereby disclaims any responsibility for them.

The author of this book does not dispense medical advice or prescribe the use of any technique as a form of treatment for physical, emotional, or medical problems without the advice of a physician, either directly or indirectly. The intent of the author is only to offer information of a general nature to help you in your quest for educational, career, and life success. In the event you use any of the information in this book for yourself, which is your constitutional right, the author and the publisher assume no responsibility for your actions.

Any people depicted in stock imagery provided by Thinkstock are models, and such images are being used for illustrative purposes only. Certain stock imagery © Thinkstock.

Printed in the United States of America.

ISBN: 978-1-5043-8272-4 (sc)
ISBN: 978-1-5043-8273-1 (hc)
ISBN: 978-1-5043-8274-8 (e)

Library of Congress Control Number: 2017909805

Balboa Press rev. date: 08/08/2019

CONTENTS

Foreword..ix

Written by Dr. Perry Wiseman

Introduction...xv

Part I: Discovery

Chapter 1: Identity—Who Am I?..5

Chapter 2: The Pull to Become…...15

Chapter 3: Purpose for Learning...28

Chapter 4: The Gap..49

Part II: Empowerment

Chapter 5: Productive and Affirmative Thinking....................63

Chapter 6: Support Team...77

Chapter 7: Organized Assets..84

Chapter 8: Closing the Gap..93

Part III: Transformation

Chapter 9: Resilience..105

Chapter 10: Open-Mindedness...117

Chapter 11: Confidence..123

Chapter 12: Self-Mastery..130

Final Thoughts 135

Theory to Practice.. 141

Assessments... 169

Resources 195

References 197

Professional Credits..205

Acknowledgments 207

About the Author..209

This book is dedicated to all educators, coaches, parents, and those who are committed to "shaping and molding" young lives for success. May you find in the pages of this book, ideas and experiences that encourage and support your intentions.

FOREWORD

by
Perry Wiseman

W HILE I HAVE unintentionally blocked out much of my early
upbringing, small snippets of that time tend to resurface
every now and then. It is difficult to describe. An event, someone,
or something small can quickly trigger a memory that has lain
dormant for many years. Of the limited recollections, though, one
particular night has not slumbered. I still recall this evening as if
it were yesterday. The date was February 9, 1986. I was an eight-
year old broken child staring out the window, curious about the
spectacle occurring miles above Earth—the Halley's Comet. Tears
were running down my cheeks. I felt hopeless.

This recollection of despair bothers me to this day (which I will
talk more about in a bit), and it has also played a role in my very
own exploration of life purpose. Is there something greater? Is there
something more exciting? This book, *No Less Than Genius,* has
challenged me to explore these exact questions—and many, many
more! The author introduces the phrase *pull to become*—which
is, generally speaking, the capability to confidently and positively
channel the perpetual internal struggles toward an exploration of
the dreams awaiting discovery.

No Less Than Genius is a guidebook to help adolescents in
their boundless journey to find a sense of meaning, direction, and

purpose. One could argue, however, that even though the book is aimed at our future—our youth—the contents of the book actually provide a road map and specific tools that are relevant to all. It has certainly challenged me.

This book is organized into three distinct parts: Discovery, Empowerment, and Transformation. This structure aligns with the current push for socio-emotional development in our young people, which is especially important with the implementation of Common Core [State Standards Initiative] as well as the push toward college and career readiness. Teaching is certainly more relational than ever. The classroom is now not just a vehicle to regurgitate content standards, but it is also a place to allow youth to explore their futures—their personal and career aspirations, their health and well-being, their true core values and motivations. Success is largely dependent on the quality of questions we ask our youth as well as the experiences and relationships we extend to them.

That said, one of the most memorable, and insightful, moments in my career came just a few months before I wrote this. Ironically, an aha moment transpired when I was about two-thirds of the way into reading this book. We had brought together fifty or so high school students from all walks of life. The ethnically diverse group of students, from nine different schools, consisted of high-achieving youth, those who were struggling, athletes, homeless youth, students with disabilities, and English learners, to name a few. This full-day experience with our young people consisted of small-group discussions around four simple (yet complex) questions, which follow:

1. Describe the very best teacher that you have had.
2. What learning experiences would you like to see that would make you excited about learning?
3. What are the most exciting possibilities for schools of the future?

4. What are your hopes for after high school, and what can we do to help you achieve your goals?

Their narratives moved hearts and minds. The room was absolutely silent as many adults and decision makers listened intently. You could hear a pin drop. Everyone heard heart-tugging truths. One young man shared his horrendous story. He sobbed as he reflected aloud about his best friend lying in his arms and breathing his last breath. Sadly, he had been shot several times in a drive-by shooting. Another scholar courageously admitted that he had been homeless for much of his life, always worrying about his next shower or even his next meal. Another young lady cried as she talked about her everyday anxiety of possibly losing her parents to deportation. Each had his or her trials and tribulations. We all have our trials and tribulations.

No matter what the story, however, there was one common thread throughout. The students were resilient. They desired to contribute to something greater. They asked for higher expectations for them. They aspired to be challenged. And they wanted to be heard. Most importantly, they spoke with conviction. One youth went on to say, "We matter. We are not these perfect little trees that are all the same height with the same exact amount of leaves; we are all different!"

They do matter. Our youth are important, and it is our collective responsibility to afford them the tools to dream big, spread their wings, and soar.

The opportunity to hear the youths' perspectives was definitely an experience that taught each educator present, including me, what we needed to learn. It was picture-perfect. Precisely, teaching and learning is more than just academia. It is, again, a relentless pursuit of building relationships and trust with our youth, guiding them to explore their current realisms, and uncovering their very own pull to become …

This book, *No Less than Genius*, does just that, by sharing precise strategies and tools to help teach our youth to acknowledge, accept, and overcome the fears that may be getting in the way of their success. Many of the ideas set forth in the book are reinforced through intimate stories from the author, riddles, and delightful fables. The first portion of the book, Discovery, provokes the reader to dig deep within. The author said, "We want to know who we really are, why we are here, and what we are truly capable of becoming and doing." This requires a cycle of deliberate questioning and reflection. What is your identity—and what is getting in the way of your dreams and espoused values?

The next section of the book is Empowerment. The reader learns clear strategies to nurture productive thinking. We have to manage and direct our thoughts proactively. Undoubtedly, this is easier said than done. Mahatma Gandhi illustrated this idea seamlessly when he said this:

> Your beliefs become your thoughts,
> Your thoughts become your words,
> Your words become your actions,
> Your actions become your habits,
> Your habits become your values,
> Your values become your destiny.

Those dreams awaiting discovery (that pull to become …, as the author has put it) require us to think and act more consciously. Simply put, our thoughts can impact our destinies.

Empowerment also includes forming strong support systems and careful action plans. We all need reliable mentors and advisors in our lives to serve as lifelines, people who offer regular guidance and support. The author references Napoleon Hill's idea of forming a "mastermind group," which is a collection of go-to people intended to help in the achievement of someone's goals and ambitions. With respect to action planning, simply writing down a plan will significantly increase the likelihood of your actually following through. Set quantifiable benchmarks. What gets measured gets done.

Transformation is the very last part of the book. Discovering yourself and empowering yourself is difficult. It takes time and effort. In this stage of the book, there is time to reflect on, and cherish, the glorious new you—the resilient, open-minded, and confident new you.

So, let's now return to the opening Halley's Comet story. Remember, the tears were running down my cheeks, and I felt hopeless. I also felt homeless because I moved a lot during those primary years. I can't even recall how many elementary schools I attended. I wouldn't be able to count them on my very own two hands. Fortunately, Grandma and Grandpa came to the rescue. They brought some stability into my life. They were my idols and I consider both of them to be my parents. They taught me how to move my dreams into reality. They instilled love, hard work (a lot of yard work, of course), and determination in me. Now I am working to impart those same values into my very own children.

There's a motivation for sharing a brief part of my personal story. It relates to the exact learnings in this book, *No Less than Genius*. While I always strive to be greater in all aspects of my life, continually refining the path forward, sometimes a dormant memory or experience can take me off track. There is a constant tug-of-war between the past, present, and future. Admittedly, there have been times (even recently) when I have deviated from my espoused path and actually let the past define me.

As a result *of No Less Than Genius*, I can now articulate and employ the many tools and strategies necessary for my personal growth. I can apply them immediately, and I am excited about teaching them to the many youth we serve, invoking their *pull to become* ...

INTRODUCTION

THE PURPOSE OF teaching is to promote learning. However, keeping youth engaged and motivated to learn has been a perpetual challenge for educators, parents, coaches, and even youth themselves. Various motivational strategies have been utilized in schools, but many teachers would agree that their effectiveness, especially using the extrinsic reward-based strategies, is short-lived at best. Even popular and more effective intrinsic strategies, such as grit and growth mindset, seem to have fallen short in some ways. For example, Duckworth's theory of grit has been criticized for idealizing hardship, especially for minority and poor children who are already showing tremendous resilience in the face of their extremely difficult circumstances. Likewise, Carol Dweck's growth mindset has also undergone serious scrutiny, not necessarily for the concept itself but for its frequent misuse in the classroom as a self-esteem booster. The concern is that when students are praised for their efforts on "busy" and mundane work lacking meaningful curriculum, purposeful teaching, and authentic assessments; this praise becomes another verbal extrinsic reward that induces only fleeting motivation. Moreover, learners know that if they are being complimented for just trying hard (effort), they must not be smart. Ultimately, "not smart" becomes a self-fulfilling prophecy that further erodes engagement, motivation, and success.

This book offers additional strategies that serve to build upon and expand the existing motivational tools available to educators, coaches, parents, and every youth.

The strategies are borne out of what the author refers to as the *pull to become* ... a maxim inspired by these five key beliefs:

- Everyone is born with a *pull to become*—the innate desire to grow, learn, and *become more* of themselves.
- This *pull to become* ... can induce a very strong motivation to engage with learning.
- All youth will succeed if educational practices promote the discovery of their *pull to become* and empower them to transform this pull to *be* and *do* into its physical reality, through a clear and definite *purpose for learning*.
- Educators, coaches, and parents can engage youth and sustain their motivation to learn by providing the support and structure necessary to actualize their unique *pull to become*....
- Leadership and administrative support for teachers' creativity and autonomy in the classroom is critical for sustained engagement, motivation, and optimized learning outcomes for youth.

These beliefs are anchored by the Self-determination theory (SDT) and framed by the concept of purpose for learning. According to Deci and Ryan (2000), SDT is a macro theory of human motivation, emotion, and development that includes factors that either support or undermine a person's natural desire to learn and grow in knowledge and understanding. Its basic tenet is that people are innately curious and have a natural love of learning that flourishes best in environments that allow autonomy, competence, and care.

David Yeager, of the University of Texas at Austin, developed the concept of purpose for learning. The idea behind this concept is to encourage youth to learn for a purpose that is greater than they are. This is because research has shown that the focus on this higher altruistic purpose for learning motivates youth to remain engaged with learning, even in the absence of immediate rewards. For example, if a student's altruistic purpose for learning is to become "a community organizer who can mobilize my community against crime and violence," then this student can connect this aim to self-generated incremental goals, such as expanding knowledge of diversity, poverty, crime statistics, community relations, public speaking and listening skills, etc., in order to achieve this higher purpose. Given that the learning goals are independently produced, purposeful and relevant to the student, he or she will be more likely to engage with the learning process and stay motivated until the realization of the goals even without external gratification.

Fusing together the perspectives of both SDT and *purpose for learning,* this book brings together in a unique way, eight mindful approaches that educators, parents, and coaches can utilize to engage, motivate, and accelerate success for every youth. The intention is to activate the dormant potentials within all youth so that they can experience success every day, in every environment - school, home, and work. The eight strategies include:

- Understanding true *identity.*
- Discovering one's *pull to become....*
- Identifying personal *purpose for learning.*
- Recognizing the *gap.*
- Practicing *productive and affirmative thinking.*
- Building *support teams.*
- Taking inventory and *organizing assets.*
- Applying assets and closing the gap with an effective *action plan.*

Even so, achieving success in any endeavor requires commitment. For this reason, families, schools, and societies that are willing to commit to incorporating these eight strategies into educating young minds will undoubtedly realize that every child is truly *No Less than Genius* as they achieve success in any quest, be it in academics, career and life itself.

This book is exceptional in that it masterfully infuses the principle of self-determination into the educational and coaching practices for youth. It does so in three ways. First, it provides a flexible curriculum that enables facilitators to create learning environments that promote autonomy, competence, and care. Second, it presents youth with an opportunity for self-exploration and discovery, thereby satisfying their innate curiosity to learn, grow, and deepen understanding of themselves and their environment. Third, it offers tools that educators, coaches, and parents can utilize to empower youth, so they can harness their knowledge and skills into a coherent, usable form that they can then apply toward the achievement of their innate pull to become. This means that rather than being told without explanation what to think and do, learners understand from an early age, the purpose for their learning. Hence, they will choose and act deliberately, with the awareness that their decisions carry consequences that matter not just to them, but also to their families, communities, and all of humanity. From this perspective, learning no longer seems like a chore but rather a meaningful undertaking that bears far-reaching consequences for self, and the elevation of human conditions. In this sense, this book may be nicknamed *the Learn, Act and Become Successful* for classrooms and homes worldwide.

The content of this book is deliberate. It is designed intentionally to fill the gap in the existing public school curriculum, which was revealed many years ago by Andrew Carnegie, as reported in Napoleon Hill's book *Think and Grow Rich*. Mr. Carnegie noted that "Schools and colleges teach practically everything except the principles of individual achievement ... they require young men and women to spend [many] years acquiring abstract knowledge, but do not teach them what to do with this knowledge after they get it." This book, *No Less than Genius* promises to take readers on a journey that reveals their pull to become—aka their *what*—which in turn informs their purpose for learning, their *why*. In other words, it guides readers toward their natural desire to *be* and *do* what matters to them with their acquired academic and experiential knowledge. The inevitable outcome of this endeavor is a heightened intrinsic motivation and engagement with learning that accelerates success for all, no matter the pursuit.

Another unique feature of this book is that it provides practical insights for educators and parents desperately seeking solutions to the challenges of student engagement, motivation, and achievement. Educators and parents who desire to rekindle the love of learning in their youth will find that this book supports their efforts. It does so by demonstrating how to tap into the source of intrinsic motivation referred to in this book as the *pull to become*. The suggested strategies included in this book will help educators and parents facilitate the process of uncovering the innate pull that is tugging at every individual, including students and scholars alike. Assisting youth to discover their unique *pull to become X, Y, or Z* is comparable to the *hook* - a strategy used to engage learners in a lesson. Guiding youth through the curriculum espoused herein and creating the environment that empowers them to become this altruistic *X, Y, or Z*, serves as the motivation to learn that inspires persistence and perseverance. Ultimately, making good grades for instance, become understood as, "for me to become an architect, so that I can design homes that are beautiful and energy efficient," and no longer "to please my teachers, parents, or impress my friends." Indeed, this ownership places the responsibility to learn directly in the hands of the learner. The more that schools and homes allow youth to own their learning, the more engaged and motivated to learn youth will be. The results will be accelerated and higher achievement, success, and fulfillment—not only in academics but also in career and life itself.

Job satisfaction for educators, especially classroom teachers, will also increase. All teachers know too well the experience of joy and satisfaction they feel when their students "get it" in class. Teachers feel more motivated and fulfilled professionally by knowing that their hard work translates to student learning and success. In like manner, a classroom full of highly motivated and engaged students is always a teacher's delight. For these reasons, this book serves to support and augment the important role of all teachers as change makers in the lives of all learners.

No Less than Genius is reader-and user-friendly. It requires only that teachers, coaches, and parents facilitate the process of self-discovery and utilize the strategies proffered to empower learners. Similarly, it is easy for learners to use, because there are no formulas to memorize, statistics to recall, poems to recite, etc. For the most part, this book simply offers deliberate and powerful strategies to engage and motivate young minds that are interested in discovering and achieving their *pull to become* more of themselves, as they achieve their dreams and contribute to society at community, local, state, federal, national, and international platforms. Other benefits to users include the following:

- It supports a focus and commitment to self-initiated goals.
- It increases constructive habits and simultaneously decreases behaviors not aligned with goals.

This book is organized around three main social-emotional themes: discovery, empowerment, and transformation. Each theme is subdivided into four sections, for a total of twelve chapters. Each chapter begins with chapter objectives, enduring understandings, and essential questions. It follows with the main content, interspersed with inspiring teaching stories. Following the twelve chapters are the author's final thoughts, theory to practice, and assessments. Finally, the book ends with resources for facilitators and other users.

PART I

DISCOVERY

Discovery is a matter of investigation and use of imagination
—Napoleon Hill

WE ARE ON the first part of our journey together. On this journey, you have the opportunity to discover your true identity, your *pull to become, your purpose for learning*, as well as the *gap* existing between your current condition, and what you are being *pulled to become*. Your interest in this exploration is natural. It is also an indication that something within you wants much more out of life. You are born curious about yourself, your possibilities, and your place in this world. So, whether you are being pulled to become the next Bill Gates, Oprah Winfrey, Mark Zuckerberg, Kobe Bryant, Michael Jordan, Cesar Chavez, Barrack Obama, or an original brand, know that your *pull to become* is achievable. Know also that it is likely to benefit not just you, but others as well. Perhaps you desire to be healthier, with more strength, stamina, and flexibility. Or maybe you are dissatisfied with the current educational system that is rife with issues of "disconnect" for many learners. Are you experiencing feelings of confusion, containment, or anxiety about your future, career, or job prospects? And what

1

about your relationships? Are they harmonious, or is there chaos and violence in the home and all around you? Whatever the case may be, your desire to be successful, peaceful, and happy give evidence that something inside of you is seeking to emerge. This *something* wants to break through, to shine, to be great. On a deeper level, this something wants to live on purpose—a meaningful life. This something is life seeking a freer, fuller, expanded expression of itself in, through, and as you—in a *big* way! Are you ready?

As humans, we are all driven by curiosity, the desire to learn and grow in knowledge and understanding. We want to know who we really are, why we are here, and what we are truly capable of becoming and doing. We all want to be successful and happy. That said, achieving anything you are being pulled to become requires that you ask questions of life. If you want a *big* life, you have to ask *big* questions and then open up yourself to receiving equally *big answers*. So, rather than have other people tell you what is or is not possible for you, be curious, and ask questions! Then quiet down, listen, and look inside of you. What you discover will amaze you. This reminds me of a parable told by Eckhart Tolle in his book *The Power of Now*. It is about a beggar who had been sitting on a roadside for many years. Rephrasing Eckhart, the story goes like this: One day, a stranger walked by this beggar. "Spare some change?" mumbled the beggar. Politely, the stranger said he didn't have anything to give, but he asked the beggar to look inside the box he was sitting on. "What's the point?" replied the beggar. "There is nothing there … just an old box. I have been sitting on it for as long as I can remember." The stranger insisted he look inside. When the beggar decided to look inside the box, what he found astonished him—the box was full of precious gems.

So are you! You are an embodiment of jewels—not as in material things, but in human qualities and capacities. That special place inside of you is full of untold possibilities. Dare to look inward— take a look inside of yourself! Though we may not have met in the physical sense, you may consider me a friend through the words I've written in this book. As a friend, I must confess that I have nothing to give you that you do not already have; I am simply reminding and encouraging you to be curious about the capacities within you for becoming … and for doing…. You are sure to discover that you are no beggar, no loser, and no failure! Rather, you are deserving, filled with unlimited potential, and quite simply *No Less than Genius!* Who you discover yourself to be because of undertaking this journey will amaze and delight you! So, come along, explore, and enjoy every phase of this adventure.

CHAPTER 1

IDENTITY—WHO AM I?

No one remains quite what he was when he recognizes himself.
—Thomas Mann

Objectives

- Learners will be able to describe their own *identity* using "I am" statements.
- Learners will be able to do a book, movie, or media production of their *identity*
- Learners will be able to summarize what they have learned in this chapter.
- Learners will be able to apply the content learned to solve a real-life problem that pertains to *identity*.

Enduring Understandings

- The thinking that one's identity is framed by one's physical appearance, environment, and experiences alone is erroneous.
- Physical appearance, environment, or experiences do not necessarily define a person, because these factors can change.
- We each have only one true identity. It is our immutable *divine* identity.

- It is important to realize that we are all more than we think ourselves to be.
- We all have an esteemed name, which is *I am* ....

Essential Questions

- Who am I and to what do I identify with?
- What if every negative thing I believe about me is false, how would I identify myself?
- What did I learn from this chapter about identity?
- How will I apply what I learned from this chapter to solve a real-life problem that pertains to identity?

College and Career Readiness Anchor Standards

- Reading Standards: R.CCR. 1, 2, 3, 4, 7, 8, 9, and 10.
- Writing Standards: W.CCR. 1, 2, 3, 4, 5, 6, 7, 8, 9, and 10.
- Speaking and Listening Standards: SL.CCR.1, 2, 3, 4, 5, and 6.
- Language Standards: L.CCR.1, 2, 3, 4, 5 and 6.

EXPLORING BIG QUESTIONS early in life has the added advantage of revealing your true identity and elevating your self-esteem early in life as well. Fortunately, you already ask big questions, such as Who am I? What am I born to be and do? These questions originate from natural desires; they are seldom arbitrary. This explains why people spend plenty of time and money seeking their identity, as we so often see on television and other media outlets. Understand that these are authentic questions that will lead you to authentic answers, depending on authentic exploration. Therefore, I encourage you to honor these questions, pay attention, and be curious about them. They come from a very special place deep inside you. That place is where your power, wisdom, and creative intelligence reside. Understand that you have unbridled access to that place, and you can go in and out of that place as often as you choose, with big or small questions. What you ask of life, backed by your belief, is directly proportional to what you get out of life! Therefore, ask the big questions! Big, high-quality questions provide equally big, high-quality answers. These hold the keys to authentic self-perception and identity in the face of labels that you or others have placed on you.

There is an African story that became permanently etched on my mind when I heard it. It is about a pregnant lioness. She is hungry, so she goes out hunting. As she wanders around the jungle, she spies a herd of goats grazing in a nearby grassland. She goes after them. She leaps and runs really fast and furiously! She closes in on the herd and, with one last desperate leap, lands right in the middle of the goat herd. Then she viciously attacks the herd, but in the process, she collapses from exhaustion. The lioness passes out and dies while giving birth to her cub. Terrified, all the goats flee, but they soon return to the same grassland to graze for food. Upon their return, they find the motherless newborn cub. In compassion, the goats decide to adopt the cub. So, this cub grows up with the herd of goats, repeating their behaviors. He bleats. He bites. He butts, and he eats grass. He believes himself to be a goat. After a year, the cub, now a one-year-old lion is wandering around the pasture with the goat herd and acting exactly like a goat.

Then, one day, a big, hungry male lion sights the goat herd and goes after them. Again, all the goats scatter in terror, except the one- year-old lion. He freezes in his tracks and stands there, just staring at the big male lion. Somehow, he senses a connection. The big lion comes over to him and says, "What's wrong with you," and admonishes him for hanging around goats and acting like them.

With indignation, the little lion declares, "I am a goat, and how is that your business?"

Ignoring the sassy remark, the big lion made several attempts to convince the little lion that he is indeed not a goat. He offers the little lion some red meat. The little one looks at the meat, hesitates, and refuses to accept it because he believes himself to be a goat. "Goats do not eat meat," "he retorted." "Goats eat grass – I, eat grass and grass only!" The big male lion insists. Out of curiosity, the little lion eventually reaches over and pulls a bite off the bone.

In this African story, when this little lion who thinks he is a goat tastes some meat for the first time, he is uncomfortable – he gags. However, when he swallows the meat, it causes him to stretch. In the process of stretching, he lets out a roar for the very first time. In this fable, this first roar is believed to be the roar of awakening. It is the point in time when the little lion recognizes that he is not who he thinks he is. He is a lion and not a goat!

Now, he realizes his true identity. From this realization, he learns that there is much more for him than his little self-perception as a goat.

And so it is with you and me. We are far more than whatever we have been conditioned to believe about ourselves. We are by far smarter, stronger, and more competent than we know. So, what is your frame? Into which category have you boxed yourself? To what do you ascribe your identity? Who do you think yourself to be? These are some of the most important questions you can ask yourself. Again, everyone, albeit to varying degrees, wonders about his or her identity throughout the various stages of life: preteen, teen, young adult, and older adult. Who are you? When you look in the mirror, are you the image you see or some other image that appears in your mind's eye? Do you like who you see, or do you turn away in self-loathing? Are you your personality, your likes, or your dislikes? Are you your feelings or emotions? Are you something someone else has said you are, or are you the opposition to something that someone else has said you are? As I was growing up, my dad always said, "Show me your friends, and I will tell you who you are." Is that true? Are you the company you keep?

Of course, the world around you is constantly saying you are this or that because it simply wants to box you into a frame, a category. The society may say you are a child or an adult and identify you by your race, ethnicity, gender, sexual orientation, socioeconomic status, political affiliation, etc. Even your parents gave you a name that probably holds some meaning for them, their culture, or their national heritage. Perhaps you identify yourself by tales of personal experiences or stories your culture and environment have told you about who you are. You use these stories as your identification card over and over again. Not long after you meet a new acquaintance, you tell your story and add, "Oh, you just don't understand. If only you know what I have been through! I am an alcoholic (or a recovering alcoholic). I am a high school (or college) dropout. I am a drug addict. I am an abused and abandoned child. I am from a dysfunctional family. I am a jailbird. Everyone in my family is in and out of jail. I am an incest survivor. I am this and I am that." The story goes on and on.

You occasionally have conversations with yourself in your head. You rehash stories about your circumstances—about your family, tribe, religion, culture, beliefs, class, or political affiliation, including your identification with or rejection of them. So, you tell all kinds of stories of past, and future as well as stories of fear, hope, anger, betrayal, sadness, joy, loss, etc. Unfortunately, these are some of the many ways by which you can identify and define yourself based on what you see, feel, hear, or think. Unconsciously, you identify with your stories and begin to let them define you. In time, you claim these stories of victimhood as your identity.

Fortunately, there is good news. And the good news is that these experiences stop defining you the moment you cease to identify with them. Even better, the definitions change—maybe not in content but at least in your perception of them. For instance, some experiences that looked horrific to you in the past may not seem that bad in the present. It isn't that the experiences did not happen, but time has a way of reshaping perception of events. So many experiences are ephemeral; they don't last, just like the morning fog that soon disappears at sunrise. But even if they do last, they are not who you are! These stories and beliefs are a form of conditioning that begins from childhood, which we internalize and carry with us as our "identity" into adulthood. They are nothing more than labels that we can peel off whenever we want.

This brings to mind the story of a young man I met at work many years ago. One afternoon, we were having lunch together at a nearby restaurant, and we got talking. He asked about my family, and amongst other things, I told him that my little boy attends the Christian school just around the corner from the restaurant. That was when he began to talk about his experience in the Christian school he'd attended as a kid. As a nine-year-old, this young man said he had been very curious and boisterous. He'd asked a lot of questions both at home and at school, and he admitted that at times he had been somewhat rambunctious. One day at school, he had started with his never-ending questions, and his teacher was fed up with his irritating behavior. So, the teacher had called him out and up to the front of the classroom. The teacher asked his classmates to take a good look at him and write him a note telling him how annoying he is, and any other thing they don't like about him. All his classmates did as they were told, and one after the other, they stood up and handed him the notes. In the notes, they wrote awful things about him - things that really hurt his feelings. They criticized his looks, the clothes and shoes he wore, the way he talked, walked, and stood. According to his teacher and classmates, everything about him was wrong and annoying – even the way he played soccer, his favorite sports. This young man narrated how he had broken down in tears and wept.

That experience had shut him down, thereafter. He became filled with anger and rage. He got into a lot of arguments and fights, and his classmates ganged up against him on the playground. Consequently, he'd withdrawn and isolated himself. His self-esteem had tanked, and he was no longer the same vibrant nine-year-old he had been. He saw himself as worthless and unlikeable. After all, if everybody, including his teacher and "friends," said he was bad and really annoying, it must be true. Therefore, he entered high school and adulthood with very low self-esteem and severe emotional pain. Lonely and emotionally scarred, he soon found comfort in food. He indulged in excessive eating into his late twenties, until he was seriously obese and ill (325 pounds at 5 foot 7 inches tall) and on the verge of losing his life. Frightened that he might die, he sought help. He checked himself into a health farm for rehabilitation. As he recalls, it was during his time in therapy that "I regained a true sense of my identity and became aware that my previous beliefs about me were erroneous." He conceded that maybe he had acted obnoxiously and that the teacher may have reacted out of frustration. More importantly though, he came to realize that the teacher was not a saint either. Neither were his classmates. He realized that the teacher was a person who'd gotten frustrated with a rambunctious nine-year-old and done something hurtful to him. Further, his classmates were simply doing what they were told by an adult. As a child, he believed all the negative comments that were made about him and internalized the hurt. Unfortunately, he had been programmed with a false identity.

In rehabilitation, this young man became aware of the many good things in, and about him. He began to understand that he is likeable, attractive, and "all-right." That there was nothing wrong with him. He knew he had made mistakes, but he also realized he was "perfect in his imperfections." Therefore, he began to value and perceive himself with a new understanding that there is a special place in him that was superlative and untarnished regardless of external conditions, emotional hurt, or even the consequences of the mistakes he had made.

That special place is also present in you—it is the core of the real you. Unlike the made-up identity or label that you have come to believe about yourself, the truth of who you really are does not change. It does not depend on your environment or experiences. No mistake can negate your true identity. This is not to deny your experiences but simply to remind you that these are not your identity. Author and New Thought Minister, Reverend Michael Bernard Beckwith puts it this way: "You are to use your experience as an initiation, a lesson, and a blessing rather than as an identity." He adds that to "identify with an experience is a misuse of that experience." Experiences are there simply to teach you what you need to learn. By all means, learn what you have to from an experience, express gratitude for what it taught you, and then let it go. An experience is not your identity.

Your real identity is *divine*—meaning that you are a *spiritual* being having a *human* experience! You must understand first of all that you are much more than your experiences, your mirror or mental image. You are more than your body, personality, feelings, emotions, etc. Yes, you have a reputation, but you are more than your reputation. You are not what you have said about yourself or what others have said you are. You are not what you have done or not done, or what others have done or not done to you. You are not the labels that you have placed on yourself or others have placed on you. You are not your stories.

Who you are is *divine*! You were created whole, complete, and perfect. You came into this world with infinite potential to be the best version of yourself that you can imagine. You were born with the natural inclination to learn, grow, and become ... You are a unique being with endless possibilities. You are one-of-a-kind brilliant, one-of-a-kind magnificent, and one-of-a-kind genius! There is nothing wrong with you - you are alright! There is nothing missing from you – you are complete! And there is nothing that you cannot be or do – anything you can see is possible for you. So, understand that this divine you is the real deal. It is the authentic you, your true identity. This is the truth of who you are, and nothing can change it, regardless of the constant change in the world around you. Even as your body undergoes physical and biological changes, your divine nature remains unchanged. Again, this changeless aspect of you is your true identity—the real you! This authentic you is far more than your body, personality, experience, condition, or reputation. The real you is spotless, a shining star—*a genius*!

If you are thinking this new identity is too good to be true, think again! It is true, it is good, and it is real, because it is unchangeable. I have heard it said that what is real does not change and whatever changes is not real. As with that little lion, so it is with you and me. When we first get introduced to the idea that we are divine—that we are spiritual beings having a human experience, that there is a genius code within us, and that we are far more than we have thought ourselves to be—we deny it! At first, we, too, get uncomfortable with this information, because it contradicts the beliefs we hold about ourselves. So, we may toss it, saying, "No, not me. *I am* ..." and describe ourselves by the personality we have identified with or by the viewpoint of those who raised us, taught us, or in some way influenced our self-perception.

Nevertheless, understand that there is something very powerful in shifting your identity from solely the human experience and expanding it to include your spiritual nature. You are a unique individual who is capable of using not only your human brain, body, emotions, and thoughts, but also your infinite mind to create and become anything you can think of. Remember that who you are is a divine being with a body, mind, and soul. You did not create yourself. You cannot even make your heart beat. You cannot take one breath on your own; neither can you make one strand of hair to grow. All of these life processes happen automatically without your input. You are this Life energy having a human experience. This Life energy lives, moves, and has its physical existence as you. This Life energy is whole, perfect, and complete. It lacks nothing! It is your true identity.

Undoubtedly, who you are is the real deal, the divine, and not the small self that is defined by worldly labels, personality, or stories. Again, this is not to deny your experiences. It's just that no matter what the experiences may be, they do not define you unless you allow them to. Your true self, the authentic self, is the self that you are before the experiences and the human and environmental conditioning. This self that is the real you has a unique purpose: to learn, grow, become more, and live the best life you can imagine. Nevertheless, you will mute that opportunity if you only identify with your stories, if you only see yourself based on the conditions that are current, known, or experienced. So, learning how to shift your perception of yourself from the limited physical perspective to the more expansive divine perspective is one of the great advantages that you have in deciding to undertake this journey of self-exploration and discovery.

On this journey, you will learn to see yourself in a different way and address yourself by a different name - your esteemed name. That name is *I am*. And how you see yourself— be it "I am genius" or "I am stupid;" "I am deserving or I am undeserving;" "I am a success or "I am a failure;" "I am powerful" or "I am powerless;" "I am a victor or I am a victim;" "I can or I can't"— will reflect the meaning you ascribe to your experiences. Remember, no experience can define you unless you give it permission. Your nature, what you are by your natural birthright, is unmuted by circumstances. As you continue on this journey, you will realize that you are far more than the things you have done or the things that others have done to you. You are not powerless but powerful. You are not a victim but a victor. You are not a villain but a hero(ine). You are not a mistake or happenstance. Neither are you the mistakes that you have made. Rather, know that you are a deliberate creation that is *No Less than Genius* in your own way. You are a person that is bright, brilliant, capable, loveable, and deserving of all good regardless of your experiences or mistakes. This, indeed, is your true identity!

CHAPTER 2

THE PULL TO BECOME...

The future you see is the future you get ...

—Robert G Allen

Objectives

- Learners will be able to articulate their *pull to become* by writing their *"what"* statements in the four domains of health, education, career or relationships.
- Learners will be able to design their *vision* or *"what"* board.
- Learners will be able to summarize what they have learned in this chapter.
- Learners will be able to apply the content learned to solve a real-life problem.

Enduring Understandings

- There is a *pull to become...* tugging at the heart of everyone.
- People may recognize this *pull to become* through their desires and dissatisfactions.
- Everyone can achieve their *pull to become...* if he or she can recognize it, decide for it, and follow up with focused action.

- For a balanced and happy life, it is important to discover one's *pull to become* in all aspects of life: health, education, career, and relationships.
- Your pull to become means your "what?"

Essential Questions

- What am I being pulled to become, and how do I know this?
- How might I visually represent my *pull to become* in the domains of health, education, career, and relationships?
- What have I learned from this chapter about the *pull to become...*?
- How might I apply what I have learned from this chapter to solve a real-life problem pertaining to my *pull to become...*?

College and Career Readiness Anchor Standards

- Reading Standards: R.CCR. 1, 2, 3, 4, 7, 8, 9, and 10.
- Writing Standards: W.CCR. 1, 2, 3, 4, 5, 6, 7, 8, 9, and 10.
- Speaking and Listening Standards: SL.CCR.1, 2, 3, 4, 5, and 6.
- Language Standards: L.CCR.1, 2, 3, 4, 5 and 6.

T HERE IS A dream tugging at your heart. This dream is just waiting for you to discover it and make it your reality. This dream is referred to in this book as your *pull to become*. It is that constant internal tug, as if there is an unseen companion constantly prodding and beckoning at you to grow, be, do, and become what you know you are here to accomplish before your time runs out on this earth. If you have not already felt this pull, quiet down and listen. You may recognize it when you "light up" simply by the thought and possibility of something. Alternatively, you may spot it when you feel constricted by a stifling job, taking classes or doing things that you find meaningless. As much as you tend to ignore the pull, it stubbornly sticks around and seldom goes away. You may suppress it, but you cannot deny its presence. It is tirelessly seeking your attention.

What are you pulled to become? Is it to become a computer scientist or a comedian? Are you pulled to become an artist, a songwriter, a pharmacist, or a fitness trainer? Whatever your *pull to become* is, understand that this is your life beckoning at you to be, do, and create whatever you can imagine. Robert G. Allen says, "The future you see is the future you get." What can you see you are being pulled to become? Are you being pulled to maintain a healthy lifestyle, make excellent grades and attend an Ivy League college, land yourself a dream job, become an entrepreneur, a philanthropist, a caregiver, build and maintain great relationships, or something else? Be curious about what is possible for you!

It is up to you to name your verb! What is your *pull to become* and do? Never mind what seems impossible and beyond your reach at this time. Imagine that all seeming limitations are removed. If you know you can't fail and that you will achieve your pull to become, what will it be for you? Go down memory lane. Think about what you loved as a kid, long before you had to worry about your safety and survival. In working with many young people, I have found that often their truest passions emerge in childhood, only to be shelved for real-life concerns. So get back in touch with these instincts, and see what comes up for you. You may begin by asking your family members, friends, or people who know you well. Ask them about when you seem the happiest and what you do enthusiastically. In addition, you may search the Internet for personal or professional heroes. Read their biographies; visit their social media sites, etc. As you search, ask yourself this question: Of everyone I know, whose career would I most want to emulate, and how could I make my unique contributions to this world? Reach out to your heroes, if possible. These actions will help to point you in the direction of your pull to become.

I read this story, *Follow Your Dream* by Jack Canfield in Chicken Soup for the Soul. It is a true story about his friend named Monty Roberts, who owns a horse ranch in San Ysidro. Often, he lets Mr. Canfield use his house to put on fundraising events benefiting youth-at-risk programs. On one of these occasions, he introduced Mr. Canfield to the audience in this way: "I want to tell you why I let Jack use my house. It all goes back to a story about a young man who was the son of an itinerant horse trainer who would go from stable to stable, racetrack to racetrack, farm to farm, and ranch to ranch, training horses. As a result, the boy's high school attendance was continually interrupted. When he was a senior, he was asked to write a paper about what he wanted to be and do when he grew up.

"That night he wrote a seven-page paper describing his goal of someday owning a horse ranch. He wrote about this dream in great detail, and he even drew a diagram of a 200-acre ranch, showing the location of all the buildings, the stables, and the track. Then he drew a detailed floor plan for a 4,000-square-foot house that would sit on the 200-acre dream ranch. He put a great deal of his heart into the project, and the next day he handed it in to his teacher. Two days later, he received his paper back. On the front page was a large red *F*, with a note that read, 'See me after class.'

"Shocked, the boy with the dream went to see the teacher after class and asked, 'Why did I receive an *F*?'

"The teacher said, 'This is an unrealistic dream for a young boy like you. You have no money. You come from an itinerant family. You have no resources. Owning a horse ranch requires a lot of money. You have to buy the land. You have to pay for the original breeding stock, and later you will have to pay large stud fees. There is no way you could ever do it.' Then the teacher added, 'If you will rewrite this paper with a more realistic goal, I will reconsider your grade.'

"The boy went home and thought about it long and hard. He asked his father what he should do. His father said, 'Look, son, you have to make up your mind on this.' However, I think it is a very important decision for you.' Finally, after sitting with it for a week, the boy turned in the same paper, having made no changes at all. He stated, 'You can keep the *F*, and I will keep my dream.'"

Monty then turned to the assembled group and said, "I tell you this story because you are sitting in my 4,000-square-foot house in the middle of my 200-acre horse ranch. I still have that school paper framed and placed over the fireplace." He added, "The best part of the story is that two summers ago, that same schoolteacher brought thirty kids to camp out on my ranch for a week. When the teacher was leaving, he said, 'Look, Monty, I can tell you this now. When I was your teacher, I was something of a dream stealer. During those years, I stole a lot of kids' dreams. Fortunately, you had enough gumption not to give up on yours.'" Jack Canfield concluded by saying, "Don't let anyone steal your dreams. Follow your heart, no matter what."

Isn't that a beautiful story? Even more appealing is the fact that it ended with an equally beautiful line: "Don't let anyone steal your dream." To this I would add, do not let any place suppress your dream—not a palace or prison cell, not paradise or purgatory. Do not let anything weaken your resolve to achieve your pull to become either—not pleasure, pain, or a perceived lack and limitation. The truth is that Monty's experience is not uncommon. Quite often well-meaning teachers, parents, relatives, and friends unintentionally quash our dreams in their desire to protect us from perceived failure. Without antagonizing these loving tendencies of relatives and friends, remember to follow your dreams, no matter what the apparent challenges.

Again, imagine that all concerns about health, education, career, money, relationships, etc. have been eliminated. If you had all the time in the world, what would you be and do? Go to the land of imagination where everything is free. While there, allow your imagination to run wild, but hold onto whatever resonates with you. Remember, in this land of imagination everything is possible—there are no limits! So, feel free to go as high and wide as you want.

After years of limiting thoughts and conditioning, I understand that this "imagining" exercise may be somewhat challenging. If you find it so, just relax, and know that you are not alone. Every time I have asked people to engage in this process, the vast majority cannot get past their mental hang-ups. As soon as they hear the questions: What are you being pulled to become? What would you love to be, do, and create? What quality of life do you see in your future? Their thoughts immediately switch to limitations; all the things they believe are barriers to achieving their pull to become. They perceive that they are being held back by family history, experiences, health situations, stories, etc. They begin thinking about what is possible for them from the perspective of limitations! Fortunately, here is the truth: there are no real limitations—except, of course, the ones you have set up in your mind. So, if you have been thinking of what is possible for you based on past or current conditions, I invite you to allow yourself to explore ideas and possibilities for a bigger and brighter future regardless of your history and current circumstances.

From experience, I have learned that your pull to become speaks to you in many ways, but most often through your desires and your dissatisfaction. So, what do you desire more of, and what are you dissatisfied with? Comedian and TV talk-show host, Steve Harvey, reminds us that "whatever we can see in our minds, we can hold in our hands." If you truly believe in your heart that you can be and have anything your mind can see or think of, that your pull – that which you are drawn to, can become your reality—the life you love living—what will you be? What do you truly believe is possible for you to achieve? What would you like to hold in your hand and experience in your life? Remember that life is full of unlimited possibilities, and it has only one agenda: to give more life, thereby expanding your perception of possibilities. So, once you decide to say yes to your *pull to become*, life simply sets in motion all that is necessary to enable you to achieve it. But you must decide. Indecision is choosing to allow others, circumstances, and situations to decide for you. This is dangerous and not in your best interest; it is the root cause of much dissatisfaction. What would you love? What are your desires? Will you decide on your *pull to become* and succeed, or will you stand on the fence and allow someone or something else to decide for you? Even worse, will you sit it out and hope for a change? Without deciding on your own *pull to become*, you face the danger of living an unfulfilled, mediocre life.

This is a wonderful opportunity to give yourself some room to explore possibilities, to begin to consider what you would love to be, do, experience, or express in four important areas of your life. The first and most important of these areas is your physical health and well-being. You are born with the desire to live and thrive. This innate desire flourishes if supported by physical and emotional wellness. So, naturally, your mind goes to work to induce activities that will keep you healthy and physically fit. If physically fit, you move around with ease and balance, and you have a healthy body weight, with not too much body fat. You have endurance, flexibility, and high energy. Physical fitness also helps you develop mental and emotional endurance. You are able to handle stress in the family, at school, work, or anywhere else. When you are physically fit, your confidence and self-esteem increase in many other aspects of your life as well: academic, work, and social interactions. You may also develop quickness of mind, alertness, and a general feeling of well-being. You are content with life as it is, and you are optimistic. You feel good, less anxious, and relaxed in knowing that everything is working together for your ultimate good. Think now about what your dream is. What do you feel pulled to become in the area of your health?

The second area is your education. What are your desires and your dissatisfactions in this area? Which subjects do you like, and which are your least favorite? Do you long to go back to school and finish your high school, college, or graduate program? Would you like to attend a trade or vocational school? How about apprenticeship and internship opportunities? Would you like to attend night school, day school, or correspondence college? Do you prefer online classes, traditional face-to face, or a combination of both? How about studying abroad? Would you like that? Whatever your preferences are, understand that both formal and informal education are equally important to your success in life. A good education opens up your mind to a world of new ideas and opportunities for growth and progress. What are you being pulled to become, and what type of education, subject matter, or academic disciplines do you desire?

The third area is your career, creativity, and your work. Are you being pulled to become an author, professional athlete, a singer, dancer, actor, teacher, doctor, lawyer, inventor, scientist, astronaut, journalist, or television personality? Maybe you desire to serve in the military, to become a barber, hairdresser, fashion designer, painter, computer scientist, technician, realtor, real estate investor, salesperson, an employer or an employee? Your choices are endless. I do not know what it is for you, but I know that there is a *pull to become...* tugging at your heart, wanting to express itself through and as you. Allow ideas to flow into you. Pay attention. Honor whatever comes up. Construct mental images of these ideas and honor the images. There's no need to worry now about how it's all going to work out, but be assured that life will support you if you decide on a dream. And because this pull is coming from your heart, it will bring work that you find fulfilling and enjoyable. What are you being pulled to become in the area of your work, career, or creative expression?

The fourth area is the relationships domain. This is the natural desire to connect with others, the need to belong. What is your desire in this area? Do you wish for harmonious relationships with family, classmates, teachers, professors, or co-workers? Do you long to meet new people and develop lasting, supportive, and respectful relationships? What about your dissatisfactions? Is there some discord in a significant relationship—say with your parents, siblings, significant others, friends, classmates, or co-workers? Remember that we have the power to create harmony in every one of our relationships. Would you like peaceful, fun-filled relationships with family, friends, co-workers, and supervisors? If you said yes to your pull to become in this area, what will it be?

Remember that the quality of our lives is largely dependent on the quality of questions we have learned to ask. For example, you could ask, I wonder how I can play in the varsity team and maintain a 4.0 GPA? Ideas that are coherent with this question will start to come to you. In other words, you become a magnet to the ideas or answers that match the questions you ask. So, in your exploration, feel free to ask simple or complex questions in the four aforementioned domains. Know that you will surely receive answers as little or as big as your questions. This is because your conscious and subconscious minds have access to the super conscious mind, where all answers reside. Be aware that these seemingly distinctive minds are essentially one mind that is separated into three categories simply for ease of communication and understanding. For instance, you may consider the mind as a computer with access to the Internet. Your conscious mind is like your desktop: you are aware of the icons on it, and you can see the task you are performing. Your subconscious mind is like the behind-the-scene programs that control how the computer works. The super conscious mind is like the Internet, the place where you can get answers to any question; it is the land of the solution! It is your genius mind, characterized by unquantifiable intelligence that knows and sees everything. Here is the good news: everyone, including you, has unlimited access to this superconscious mind that is the source of all knowledge, information, people, connections, and other resources you will need on this journey of exploration, discovery and becoming. Thus, what questions are you asking? What are you being pulled to become in the areas of your health, education, career, and relationships? Are you listening for answers? Take a deep breath, do some reflection, open up, and allow ideas to flow in freely. Write down or draw images of what you are being pulled to become in these four important aspects of your life.

It is decision time! Your life—my life, everyone's life—is about a series of decisions. You either make them consciously or others make them for you unconsciously, but you can't avoid making a decision. If you do nothing, then you have consciously decided that you are okay with whatever comes your way. On the other hand, if you decide to yield to your *pull to become*, you are focused and deliberate in your actions. In this manner, you are more likely to achieve your goals in accelerated time and live the life you are truly happy to live.

To illustrate the importance of deciding for a *pull to become*, I am reminded about a student who walked into a classroom at the beginning of a semester. He walked up to a professor and said, "Professor, I registered for this class. Will you give me a good grade?" The professor looked up at the student, reached into his cabinet for the grading rubrics, and said, "Certainly, I will give you a good grade. Just tell me what grade you want, and I will let you know what you have to do to earn the grade you say you want."

The student kind of froze, surprised by the professor's response, and said, "Sorry, Professor, I can't tell you that. If I do, you might make me do a lot of work, and then, who knows, you may decide not to give me the grade I want after all."

The professor said, "Well, young man, here is how it works. You tell me the grade you want, and you do the work for that grade. It's that simple, and it is school policy."

The student insisted, saying, "Professor, I fully understand what you are saying. However, it is important for me to let you know that

I am apprehensive about it. I don't want to do the work, hand it over to you, and then you'll be holding my work and my grades."

The professor said, "Young man, I will give you the grade for the work you do. Again, that's school policy! You have to go along with school policy." The student and the professor continued to argue in this fashion. Exasperated, the professor said, "Young man, I'm sorry. I am not going to be able to assist you under this circumstance. Please leave. Go register for another class or try something else." So, the student left. He went to another professor and repeated the same behavior. Again, he was turned away.

Relentless, he went to a third professor. He was going through the same routine with the professor, explaining how he did not want to specify the grade or do the work before he got the grade he wanted. Finally, the young professor, who had now lost his patience with the student, reached under his desk, pulled out a manila folder, reached across and smacked the student on the head, saying, "Here is the rubric—decide on a grade!"

Startled, the student picked up the grading rubric, looked it over, decided on a grade, and handed it back to the professor. Classes began. The student kept his commitments as laid out in the rubrics. He did the required work, and he got his desired grade at the end of the semester. Feeling very successful, he registered for the first professor's class the following semester. Again, he walked up to the professor, and he said, "Look! In that class I got the grade I wanted." The professor answered, "That may well be, but even in that class, I am sure that you had to decide on a grade first, commit to it, and complete the required work before you received the grade."

The student agreed with the professor, but added that "no instructor ever explained it to me quite like that professor did."

I smile to myself every time I remember this story. This is because something within me recognizes that this story is not unique to this student. Somehow, it is my story and perhaps yours as well. Essentially, we approach life and we say, "Will you please give me my dream—my pull to become?"

To that, life says, "Sure, I will! Tell me exactly what you know you are being pulled to become —be specific! Detail your desire, your dream, and your yearnings. Clarify and decide! Put your name on this pull to become. Put your whole self into what you desire; lean into it with your whole being; claim it with your words and actions; commit to it, and I will support you so you can actualize this specific pull to become."

Our answer is, "Wait a minute! I do not want to commit just yet. What are the guarantees, anyway? In fact, I do not have the time. I am too busy right now. But give me my dreams first, and later, I will commit and figure out what to do and when." Now, imagine you have a rich and generous uncle who has recently passed away. In his WILL, he has bequeathed to you $525,000 which you are free to spend any way you like. This is definitely a lot of inheritance for many people. If this really happened to you, how would you spend your money?

The truth is that each and every one of us, including those you think or know to be successful, have exactly this same inheritance. It is called the gift of time. Like everyone else, you have a little over 525,000 minutes in the twelve months that make a year. If we all live twelve more months, each one of us will inherit this same amount of time, which we are free to invest any way we choose. How will you use your time? Will you invest it on rehashing past mistakes and perceived failures, nursing a problem, harboring a resentment, or just waiting and hoping? Using your time in any one of these ways is counterproductive!

You want to invest your time and energy on recognizing your *pull to become...*, committing to it, and taking action for it, and not against it. Remember, we all have the capacity to *be* and *do* bigger and better things with our lives. So, decide on your *pull to become...*, and begin to invest your time toward achieving it in these four important areas of your life: health, education, career, and relationships. Again, draw or write down the images or ideas that come to mind. Be reminded that a large body of research affirm that doing so increases the likelihood that you will place its achievement at the top of your priority list.

In closing, remember that life is constantly calling on you through your pull to become! No one is exempt. You can either yield to this pull or ignore and resist it. The decision is yours. Nevertheless, understand that the choices you make bear far-reaching consequences for your learning, personal growth, development, success and fulfilment in life. If you say yes to this pull, learning becomes meaningful and personally rewarding. If you ignore it, learning could become boring, impersonal, and meaningless. If you resist it, learning could become frustrating and annoying. So, here is an opportunity to begin the process of exploration, discovery, and decision for your *pull to become*. Thus, this book is more than just another text to read! It is a road map to guide you toward the achievement of your *pull to become* ..., and to help you create community or global impact with this *pull* in a way that benefits you and the rest of humanity.

CHAPTER 3

PURPOSE FOR LEARNING

The purpose of learning is growth, and our minds, unlike our bodies, can continue growing as we continue to live.
—Mortimer J. Adler

Objectives

- Learners will be able to write a paragraph to articulate the meaning of *purpose for learning*.
- Learners will be able to articulate in writing, their *purpose for learning* statement, aka their "*why*" statement, reflect on, analyze, and revise this statement to ascertain that it is worthy of their commitment.
- Learners will be able to summarize what they have learned in this chapter.
- Learners will be able to apply the content learned to solve a real-life problem that pertains to *purpose for learning*.

Enduring Understandings

- Everyone has a unique *purpose for learning*.
- Understanding your *purpose for learning* keeps you engaged and motivated to learn.

- Reflecting on your values and pull to become guide your decisions and keep you focused on your *purpose for learning.*
- Testing the validity of your *purpose for learning* is an important way to determine whether your purpose is worthy of your commitment.
- Your purpose statement is a living document and should be written in present tense—as the commitments you are making now.
- Your purpose for learning is your *"why?"*

Essential Questions

- What is *purpose for learning?*
- How might I articulate the *purpose for learning* that is right for me?
- What did I learn from this chapter?
- How might I apply what I have learned to solve a real-life problem that pertains to *purpose for learning?*

College and Career Readiness Anchor Standards

- Reading Standards: R.CCR. 1, 2, 3, 4, 7, 8, 9, and 10.
- Writing Standards: W.CCR. 1, 2, 3, 4, 5, 6, 7, 8, 9, and 10.
- Speaking and Listening Standards: SL.CCR.1, 2, 3, 4, 5, and 6.
- Language Standards: L.CCR.1, 2, 3, 4, 5, and 6.

P EOPLE, ESPECIALLY CHILDREN and youth, are very curious about the world around them, and how they fit in. Many classroom teachers and other adults working with young people have reported that when required to perform certain tasks or assignments, students frequently do ask these questions: Why am I doing this? What does this have to do with my future, and how will it help me achieve my goals, as well as what I want to be and do? Indeed, these are valid questions that deserve the attention of educators, parents, and coaches everywhere. Such questions need to be explored, not just by youth but also by adults in every walk of life because they speak to the issue of relevance, personal meaning, and purpose for learning or living.

Now, if you have dared to ask these or similar questions of your teachers, parents, mentors or coaches, I wonder whether you were always truly satisfied with the responses you received. My guess is that you were not! The reason is this: these are very personal questions that no one else can answer for you. This implies that each one of us must answer these questions for ourselves in order to discover our purpose or our why in life, business, education, etc. If you are a student, exploring these questions offers a great opportunity for you to align your *purpose for learning* with your *pull to become*. For example, if you are pulled to become an architect, your purpose for learning may trigger these questions: Why do I want to be an architect? Why am I taking so many classes—English, history, other humanities, mathematics, physics, and sketching, etc. Why will my becoming an architect matter to my family, community or society?

In response, your *purpose for learning* statement could be, I am studying to become an architect in order to design energy-efficient buildings that will help families and businesses reduce energy costs and maximize profits respectively. In this sense, your purpose for learning becomes a mission that has some benefit not just for you but for others as well. *Purpose for learning* brings meaning, relevance, focus, and ownership to your learning.

This excerpt from a poem by Russell Kelfer underscores the notion that our contributions matter and that we are created equipped with the appropriate skills and talents to achieve our purpose for learning or living.

> You are who you are for a reason,
> You're part of an infinite plan.
> You are a precious and perfect unique design,
> Called ... [a] special woman or man.

This poem is a reminder that you are not an accident; you are not in this world by chance. You were created as part of a grand design for life right here on earth. You have unique gifts and talents that are tailor-made for you, so you can contribute to this magnificent design of life. This design will be incomplete without you. You are a co-creative partner with life. There will never be anyone just like you to walk the face of this planet. Thus, no one can take your place and contribute to this grand design just the way you would. You know that your life has meaning; it is significant, and your purpose for learning is to honor your pull to become (i.e., achieve whatever it is that you are being pulled to become). Having discovered your pull to become in the previous chapter, it is your responsibility to now focus your learning in alignment with it so that it becomes your reality ... the meaningful life you truly love living.

For those of you who have discovered your purpose for learning, regardless of the learning environment—school, work, or life itself—this purpose will remain the guiding force in your life. It will give you direction, clarity, and focus. It will inform your decisions. It will energize and keep you engaged and motivated, even when the going gets tough. If you know your purpose for learning, schoolwork gets easier and less complicated. You are happier learning even difficult subjects, because these have meaning for you. You feel inspired, enthused, and engaged with school and the learning process. Work or school becomes less of a chore and more of an opportunity for growth. In fact, your *purpose for learning* paves the road to your success in school, career, and life itself.

I am humbled to share with you how I discovered my *pull to become,* and my *purpose for learning* and living. As I was born around mid-March of 1960, astrologers would say that my birth date points to what they call "Life Path 1." Amongst other things, Life Path 1 suggests that people feel safe around me and are drawn to me. They seem to trust my judgments and value my opinions. I am quite often the go-to person when comrades need words of encouragement. Although hardly interested in astrology, I have to admit that some of their predictions parallel my life experiences. I was born into a family that adored me and showered me with unconditional love. As a result, I grew up feeling safe, confident, and happy. People say I am good natured, friendly, kind, generous, compassionate, forgiving, and nonjudgmental. Perhaps these qualities make it easy for friends, family, colleagues, or even strangers to share some of their deepest secrets with me. On my part, I have done my best to honor these personal stories, even as early as in grade school. And guess what? I come alive when I have the opportunity to offer support and encouragement to those in need, especially when they feel alone and vulnerable.

As indicated earlier, I had a very happy childhood experience. In my recollection, there was hardly any typical childhood or adolescent challenge—issues like poor self-image, the feeling of not being good enough, rejection, isolation, loneliness, bullying, etc. that I couldn't handle. Of course, I knew how to make things happen for me! I felt in control of every aspect of my life. My parents would be among the first to admit that they saw this independent spirit in me when I was a child and learned to "leave me alone" at a very young age. So, in my young mind, I believed that life was not only good, but also, easy and predictable. I carried this mental and emotional orientation through high school and college.

It was not until after I got married at the age of twenty-three that I began to view myself and my perception of life differently. The first shift occurred when I experienced my first miscarriage of pregnancy. The blow was a low and devastating one, accompanied by an overwhelming feeling of emptiness. After I recovered somewhat, I thought, okay, this has to be a fluke! It's a major knock, nevertheless, but I can handle it—I am still in charge of me! So, to regain control, I quickly put things in perspective, waited a year, and tried again. Then a second one happened! This time, the familiar gut-wrenching blow hit me with an amplified intensity that brought me to my knees. I collapsed in agony and despair. I could no longer be in denial. I was losing control. Without a doubt, something beyond my awareness was now in charge of my life. I cried and I prayed for help and understanding. I also began to get curious—to really be attentive to my experiences.

However, by the time the third serial miscarriage happened, all rationality was out the door. As I held my lifeless twenty-eight-weeks- gestational twins in my hands, my whole world collapsed, just like their underdeveloped lungs. Self-annihilation seemed the only option. I wanted to die! My paradigm was shattered beyond recognition. The bottom had fallen out, and my life was in a vicious downward spiral. It was spinning out of my control. My life felt hollow and meaningless. Then and only then did I really concede that I had never truly been in total control of anything, not even my life, as I had previously thought.

These harrowing experiences saddened and constricted me. They also left me confused and powerless. For the first time in my life, I felt vulnerable, deflated, and mangled by life! I cried out for help, but no one heard me! I wanted answers to my questions: What do these experiences mean? Moreover, what am I supposed to do now? How do I move forward when I have no strength? The power that was now in charge of my life was definitely beyond my understanding. Undoubtedly, it was a greater power. Despite my pain and distress, I was determined to discover what this power was, for two main reasons. First, then I could at least bow down and surrender to it, and second, maybe I could cooperate with it for the sake of my own happiness. Indeed, life as I now knew it was neither easy nor predictable. Life was brutal! Yet, somewhere really deep inside of me, I felt the love of life, its warmth and comforting embrace, even when peace seemed distant.

So, with curiosity, I set out for a new beginning, in search of meaning and purpose for my life. In essence, I was in search of my *what* and my *why*. I gave up everything—my marriage, my home, and my flourishing career as a petroleum geologist—and left for the United States, the land of freedom and opportunities for self-exploration and expression. In mid-summer of the late eighties, I arrived in California with $250, the clothing on me, a few pictures, and some personal letters. I lived with my sister for about a year, saved money earned from my jobs as a food- and customer-service associate, and then moved out on my own.

Since then, I have acquired graduate and postgraduate degrees in education. I am happily remarried, a mother, and the holder of a full-time job as a high school teacher. I have also held a position as an adjunct professor at a local university. I make a comfortable living, dwell in a neighborhood and house that I love, drive the car of my dreams, travel, and enjoy the company of my family and good friends. Honestly, I love my life!

Even so, there was an aspect of me that still felt unfulfilled at that time, a vacuum. I recognized that the pull that had brought me to America—the search for meaning in my life—was only partially accomplished. Materiality had never been an issue. Motherhood? Thankfully, I am now a mother. Yet, I still felt as if something were missing. A deeper inward search revealed the burning desire to find more meaning in my work. Over two decades of experience in the classroom had taught me the power of purposeful teaching and learning. I felt pulled by the need to grow, serve, be, and do more with this knowledge. I wanted to make a significant contribution to the field of education. More importantly, I desired to connect my students' *what and why* with teaching so as to improve learning outcomes for all of them.

I was dissatisfied with the status quo—an educational system that failed to teach students what success truly meant and how to achieve success in, and beyond the classroom. I liked giving encouragement and support. I believed that students deserved the opportunity to discover and identify their unique purpose for learning. I saw that they needed to make sense of what was being taught and know why they ought to learn it. It was my belief that they needed a multi-level system of support that address their academic, behavioral, as well as their social-emotional needs to prepare them adequately for success in college, career, and the challenges/opportunities of life. At the same time, I was acutely aware that the academic standards (even with its merits), and rigid school calendar often restricted teachers' autonomy to be flexible and creative in the classroom.

Although jobs outside the classroom were always viable options, I never seriously pursued any. I believed deep inside of me that some of the changes I was seeking must come from me, as an educator inside the classroom. Moreover, I loved the interaction and exchange of ideas with my students. I was energized by their youthfulness. Their spontaneity often helped me to "go with the flow." Their wit, coupled with their keen senses of humor, helped me laugh out loud. Even their antics and follies touched a special place in my heart that reminded me of how I used to be. I loved to hear the response, "Oh, now I get it!" as well as the aha moments. When I acknowledged their contributions, I loved the experience of seeing their eyes light up and broad smiles appear on their faces. At that instant, their body posture would shift to convey a sense of power and confidence that I found really gratifying. For the most part, these and many other anecdotal classroom experiences left me wondering about the genius potential that lay dormant within my students, and all youth for that matter. I was curious about the awesome things they could be and do given deliberate support and structure. Most importantly, I thought about how I could increase their motivation and engagement with purposeful learning.

My experiences in the field of education have caused me to realize that we have a long way to go in order to fulfill the real purpose of education. The aim of education, in my opinion, is to enable individuals achieve at their highest potential engendered by the discovery of their pull to become, and their unique purpose for learning. Fulfilling this aim for all learners remain elusive partly because most educational policies and practices still weigh heavily on academic competencies without emphasizing the personal relevance of acquiring this knowledge. For instance, one of my colleagues, a history and social science teacher, recalls a student asking, "How does learning about dead people in some countries I do not know or even care about help me become a politician?" Perhaps, this may sound naïve, but what is noteworthy is that questions of this nature give evidence to the disconnect that sometimes exists between the school curriculum and the learner.

Undoubtedly, as long as youth continue to sense this disconnect and the absence of personal relevance in the curriculum taught, the lack of motivation to engage with the learning process will remain a perpetual challenge for educators, especially classroom teachers. Moreover, many off-task behaviors evident in classrooms will persist without effective motivational strategies. This realization generated within me more of the familiar unresolved feelings of constriction, frustration, and curiosity about the meaning of my work and life as a whole. Therefore, I began to ask questions again. What was life trying to teach me with my convoluted experiences—a happy childhood, a mixed bag of joy and pain, and both success and failure as an adult? Why do my life and work experiences seem and feel disjointed? What if I could merge both into a meaningful whole? What might it look like? How might I even begin?

Unable to understand the incessant tug of life's highs and lows, I prayed, meditated, and embarked on my own inward journey of self- exploration. I wanted to really find out for myself the reason for my existence on this planet - the purpose of my learning and life. Then one day, as I was driving home from work, the epiphany came! It came as a still, small voice that said to me, "all is well! Know that you are whole and complete. Your life experiences and work are coherent. In fact, all your experiences—the highs as well as the lows—are in order. They are working together to prepare you for a greater good. Remember how you have always been there for anyone going through tough times? Remember the details of your previous job as a petroleum geologist, when you worked in remote field locations, under hostile weather conditions? You gathered data and used the data to explore and produce crude oil, a highly valued natural resource that resides deep within the earth. Your work then was service to humanity. You did the same in your temporary jobs as a sales and customer-service associate ... you served people by quickly helping them locate food and other items they needed. That, too, was service to humanity. As a teacher, you are helping students discover the highest possibilities within them and empowering them to turn these possibilities into their realities. In your classroom, you give students autonomy—voice and choice about their learning—and you help them feel competent in their ability to learn. More importantly, you show them that you care about them, and they know it! Thus, you are providing the environment for them to stay motivated and engaged with learning. Helen, your calling has always been to serve humanity as an encourager. Your life and work experiences have prepared you well, but there is more. And this is what you are being called to be and do next: be a dream support coach for young people. Use your experiences in and out of the classroom to empower youth define and achieve success on their terms."

Whew! My life purpose for all my learning—school and experiences—had just been revealed to me in a most lucid form! Was I relieved? This encounter left me with goose bumps all over my body. I took a moment to express gratitude to this voice, which was now faint and almost inaudible. With a clarity of purpose, I could not be happier or more motivated. Since then, I have surrendered all notions of personal control and yielded to this pull to become an encourager and dream support coach for youth. This pull has informed my purpose for learning and living, which led to the writing of this book and the incorporation of a company dedicated to accelerating success for youth: Support & Structure Coaching, LLC.

Essentially, the purpose for writing this book is to offer strategies that facilitators can apply to help youth discover their *pull to become* and to keep them engaged with purposeful learning, so that they can achieve success in accelerated time, while doing the things that really matter to them.

What is your purpose for learning or living? What is your why? I discovered mine in a roundabout way, in late adulthood, after a mixed bag of personal challenges and breakthroughs. Many adults look back at their lives and wish they had discovered their life purpose earlier, so they could have lived more purposeful and intentional lives and done the work that really mattered to them. Although it is never too late, many wish they had the opportunity that is available to you right now—to explore and discover their purpose for learning and living earlier in life, instead of going around in circles, as I did. Surely, if they'd found meaning early in their lives, many believe they could be living a life of more focus, fulfillment and happiness.

Fortunately for you, you are young, and you don't have to lead an adult life full of regrets or wishes unfulfilled. Here is your opportunity to focus on becoming and doing what your heart pulls you to be and do. Here is your chance to discover and focus on the purpose for learning that supports you and what you are created to be and do. Discovering how to allow your purpose for learning to guide you and keep you motivated and engaged with learning (in and out of school) is one of the many benefits of this book. This knowledge will enable you to achieve your dreams and do work that is meaningful to you.

Having discovered your *pull to become* in the previous chapter, your *purpose for learning* is hopefully clearer. Be assured that you will gain even more clarity as you stay engaged with this book and the strategies it proffers. Applying the strategies will help you find meaning in school or work and will motivate and engage you with learning in any situation.

To sustain a high level of engagement and motivation, it is imperative that you test your *purpose for learning* from time to time. You need to know whether this purpose—your why—is right for you and that you are not trying to please someone else or go with the current fad. Understand that your purpose for learning must support your pull to become which is tugging at your heart. You have recognized this pull, said yes to it, and you have decided for it. Now that you have committed to it, some doubts may begin to pop up in your head. You may begin to question whether you can really fulfill this purpose. Likewise, you may even wonder whether you are deserving of this pull to become a bigger and better version of yourself. If you are experiencing these hallmarks of hesitation and self-doubt, I encourage you to relax and realize that you are not alone. Every successful person encounters feelings of apprehension sometimes. So, when these questions or similar concerns arise, I suggest that you practice what I learned from a mentor and wise friend: ask a more empowering question! Ask whether this purpose for your learning is worthy of you and your time, talent, and commitment. Remember, you are going to give this *purpose for learning* your all, so it had better be meaningful for you, not someone else.

Following is a six-point tool to test whether your *purpose for learning* is right for you.

1. Does my *purpose for learning* line up with my pull to become?

This question brings to mind a story that a friend shared with me at a graduation party. It was about a successful constitutional lawyer who had just been appointed as a federal judge. To celebrate this accomplishment, his friends had a party in his honor. Although everyone was having fun, this guy appeared aloof and sad. This prompted a friend to seek explanation for the cause of his aloofness and sadness, especially since he achieved something that many people could only dream about by becoming one of the nation's most revered judges.

Responding, the judge lamented the fact that he achieved something that he did not even want. Further, he indicated that he had absolutely no intention of even being in the legal profession in the first instance and that he now felt chained to the profession that he did not like.

The judge's friend was bewildered. He could hardly believe what he had just heard. Then, he opined that his friend had one of the highest honors in the judicial arm of government. Moreover, he noted that the judge's wife and children are comfortable and happy, and that all his friends are elated for him and have the highest respect for him. So, he wondered aloud what more anyone could ever want.

Without hesitation, the judge responded, saying that what was of utmost importance to him was self-respect. He stated that he did not respect himself because he yielded to what his loved ones want for him and ignored his own desires. He added that what he really wanted beyond anything else was to become a dancer and teach dance to young people. His parents were against this, and he listened to them. The judge felt that this showed weakness on his part, and that although he became a revered judge, he was however only mediocre in the field that he wanted to dedicate his life to. He concluded that this was the main cause of his unhappiness.

When I heard this story, I felt sorry for the judge. In spite of his outward success, he remains in a lonely and miserable situation because his purpose for learning is out of sync with his pull to become. Frankly, I would not have liked to be in his shoes, and perhaps you may not want to be in his shoes, either. Unfortunately, there are many people who spend time pursuing goals that are not theirs. They nevertheless achieve them, but they also end up unhappy and unfulfilled. So, be mindful - it is very easy for anyone to slip into a similar situation. You want your *why* to line up with your *what*. This means you want your *purpose for learning* to line up with your *pull to become*—something you really want to be, do or have, and not what others want for you. When you think of your *purpose for learning*, does it line up with your pull to become?

2. Does my *purpose for learning* align with my core values?

Your core values are the things that matter to you. They include thought patterns and beliefs that make you feel real, authentic, whole, and complete. Some examples include self-reliance, family, adventure, freedom, commitment, responsibility, loyalty, love, service, etc. These are only a few examples of core values and beliefs that people hold. Perhaps you share some of these values, but because you may not always be aware of your beliefs, it is imperative that you look inside of you to determine what your own values are. Knowing and honoring your core values is essential in order to sustain commitment to your learning, being, and doing. On the contrary, not knowing or adopting values that are convenient or that seem to work for others is a bit like following the Joneses— inauthentic. The values are not yours, and you will never really feel genuine when you live by adopted values.

When your purpose for learning is aligned with the things that matter to you, internal conflicts diminish, you are less confused, you are at peace with the decisions you make, and you experience life as stress-free, even as you work toward achieving your pull to become. Be encouraged and relax with the knowledge that the *purpose for learning* that is right for you will always be coherent with your core values. This *purpose* will never require you to do something that contradicts your core values. With this in mind, I encourage you to do what matters to you and what you truly believe in your heart to be right for you.

Here is a story about a young man I had the privilege to work with. This young man was at a crossroad when he came to speak with me. His purpose for learning was to fulfill his dream of becoming a military personnel so he can serve his country and fellow citizens, just as his father had done. Unfortunately, his father had been killed in combat during the Iraq War. This young man had barely known his father because he'd been only four years old when his dad was deployed. However, he learned a lot about his dad from his mom. According to mom, his dad had been a dedicated father, a loving and supportive husband, and an honorable man. So, this young man grew up with great admiration for his dad. And when he made the cut and was recruited into the army, his purpose for learning was in perfect alignment with his core value to serve and protect his country and fellow citizens.

However, something within him did not feel right. He was concerned about his mom. As an only child and because of his dad's early transition, he had been very close to his mom. Growing up, he had witnessed firsthand how much his mother missed his dad. On numerous occasions, he'd heard her crying for his dad behind closed doors. So, this young man grew up wanting to be near his mom, to provide for her and protect her, just as he imagined his dad would have done. But when this young man came to me, he said, "My purpose for learning is to fulfill my pull to become a military personnel so that I can serve and protect my fellow citizens and country. Now that this purpose seems in perfect alignment with what I am being pulled to become, I am very concerned that I might be deployed outside the country after my training. This would take me far away from my mom. She would be alone, and then I would not be able to care for her in her old age. I do not know what to do."

After listening attentively, I asked him to go back and explore other possible versions of service to community and country. "What are the different ways that you can serve?" was the question I posed to him. "You see, whenever you are not settled about something— be it a decision, a choice, or an action—it is a signal that there is a disconnect from your core values. Therefore, you need to do a revisit, to go back, to reflect, and get curious about the disconnect and the dissatisfaction." So, he left, and we talked a couple of weeks later. This time he looked a lot better; his shoulders were held back, there was more bounce in his step and a big smile brightened his face. You can tell when someone feels good; it shows in their demeanor.

"So," he said, "You know, as you instructed me, I have been thinking about the different possible versions of service. Although many versions came to mind, my favorite is to become a firefighter.

As a firefighter, I can serve others and country by saving lives, homes, and properties. At the same time, I can be near my mom and make enough money to take good care of her." As he said this he lit up, and I could tell that this was a purpose that aligned with his core value of service to family, community and country.

I urge you to recognize that this is possible for you, too. When your purpose for learning is in alignment with your core values, you will light up with your decisions, and the gut-wrenching conflicts will diminish.

Years later, I met this young man at a grocery store. By this time, he was now twenty-five years old, and he had accepted a position as a firefighter in a nearby city eight months earlier. He loves his job, he was serving his community and country, and best of all, he is able to be there for his mom. His pull and purpose are aligned with his core values.

You want to make sure your purpose for learning aligns with your deep-seated values and beliefs.

3. Is my *purpose for learning* big enough that it requires that I grow and expand my capacity for more learning?

As you reflect on this question, consider the message in this story. It was Christmas time, and for Christians, it is a season of joy, gratitude and appreciation. For children, it is, in addition, a time when Santa Claus is expected to shower them with gifts. On the days leading up to Christmas, many families would take their children for Christmas shopping. Once, a family took their six-year-old daughter to a popular shopping center. Present at that mall was Santa Claus giving away Christmas goodies. The little girl went up to Santa to receive presents. She held out a small jar, and Santa filled her small container with goodies. Excited, she showed her parents the candies, and even proceeded to count them. But her spirit soon dampened when she noticed that the girl beside her got a lot more treats than she did. She desired more goodies.

A couple of days later, the family attended another event where Santa Claus was present. Again, the little girl walked up to Santa with the same small jar, and once again, Santa filled her small jar with goodies. Curious about how many treats she received this time, she proceeded to count her candies and discovered she received exactly the same amount as she did two days earlier. She also observed that other kids around her received much more. This happened a third time. However, by the time this little girl discovered for the fourth time that many other kids received more treats from Santa, she wondered why. Then, she said to her parents: "Dad, mom, have I been good? Do you think Santa likes me? Why does Santa always give me less candies than other kids although I desire to have more?"

To these questions, the parents reassured her that she had been good all year and that Santa knows it too. The problem is that she had been going to Santa with a small container. They encouraged her to get a large jar and to notice what happens. So, the next time they were at a mall the girl did exactly as she was told. She walked up to Santa with a large container. To her pleasant surprise, Santa Claus filled the large container with more candies than she had ever hoped for.

Isn't that interesting? As simple as this story may appear, it bears with it a profound truth about life: life will only give you as much as you are willing to receive. So how big is your purpose for learning? And, by how much are you willing to stretch yourself, grow in knowledge and understanding, so that you may expand your capacity to accommodate this grand purpose? Remember that life placed your pull and purpose in your heart because it knows you have the capacity to achieve it. Not only that, life will support you all the way. However, you have to want it. Like the six-year old, you have to want it bad enough that you are willing to ask big questions that will expand your capacity for more learning. The status quo – business as usual - the small jar isn't big enough. You will need to get a "bigger ja r."

This girl's experience is not unique to only children. Many youth, and even adults often act in similar ways unconsciously.

Life, like Santa Claus, offers the possibility of a big, purposeful, and successful life – the very things we desire. And rather than make the effort to get a bigger container (grow, learn and expand our capacity to achieve this possibility) we make excuses to ourselves, *"Not me! I am not good enough. I do not have the intelligence nor the time. I am too young, (too old, fat, skinny, tall, short, etc.).* In fact, my current performance level in reading, writing, and speaking are not high enough, and cannot support this big *purpose for learning.* It is just too much work; the learning curve is too steep; Santa or life may never give me a break. So, what's the point? Why go through the hassle of reaching out to seek a bigger container?" Consequently, we get discouraged and may give up on our *purpose for learning.* We settle for less and choose lower instead of higher. And we inadvertently say to life: "give me a smaller *purpose for learning,* something that I can handle with my small container." Unfortunately, life responds accordingly, and we keep going home with the same small goodies – a mediocre level of achievement instead of the huge success that is possible for us. There is no growth associated with this way of thinking; there is only stagnation and decay.

So here is a suggestion: whenever life places in your heart a big purpose, rise up to the occasion – get a bigger container. If a six-year-old can do it, so can you. This means stretching your thinking, opening up to new ideas, reexamining old ideas, and working harder and smarter—so that you may grow and expand your capacity to receive more wisdom, guidance, and understanding that can enhance your success.

4. Would my *purpose for learning* further develop my skill sets or assets?

Your assets are your strengths or strong points. In general, they come in two categories: transferable and technical. Your transferable skills are those that will serve you well regardless of your pull to become and purpose for learning. Some examples of transferable skills include critical thinking, collaboration, good communication, creativity, ability to organize, resilience, open-mindedness, confidence, self-mastery, etc. This list is by no means exhaustive. Feel free to explore and find your own. If you don't already know your personal strengths, explore the work of Seligman and Peterson (2004). These scholars suggested ten criteria with which to determine whether a trait is a strength of yours. These criteria are paraphrased as follows: (i) you identify with the trait, (ii) you are excited while using it, (iii) you easily learn things related to it, (iv) you explore new ways to use this trait, (v) you are eager to act in agreement with this trait, (vi) you can't be dissuaded from using it, (vii) you are seldom tired or bored when using this trait, (viii) you seek work pertaining to this trait, (ix) you create work that requires this trait, and (x) you are intrinsically motivated to use this trait. So now you have it! Put your perceived strengths through this ten-point test to determine which ones you really own and which ones you want to develop.

Your technical skills include specialized knowledge acquired from schooling, internship, volunteer opportunities, etc. Some examples include playing a musical instrument, recording sounds, court reporting, processing x-rays, arranging flowers, driving a truck, testing water quality, painting, etc. Explore, and keep a record of all the skills you have acquired through formal and informal education. Your purpose for learning should help you hone your skills and assets.

5. Does my *purpose for learning* require that I seek help?

Your purpose for learning typically requires that you step out of your comfort zone to that place called the "unknown" territory. This unfamiliar territory may be very uncomfortable and scary. Therefore, understand that you are going to need help to navigate this unfamiliar terrain. No one knows everything. If you ever feel you know everything there is to know about your purpose for learning, also know for sure that your purpose is not big enough. Therefore, in order to fulfil your purpose for learning, it is imperative that you seek help. The six-year old turned to her parents – people she knows and trust. If you are surrounded by trusted family and friends, it is okay to turn to them for help. If not, know that self-help is also available. Trust your inner guidance system (gut feeling) for instructions on the next step to take and for the courage to forge through and move forward despite doubts. For instance, this might mean that you have to develop grit, to persevere in your desire to learn not only the difficult subjects, but also the ones you do not like but know are important to your purpose. This might also mean that you have to re-evaluate how and what you spend your time doing. You might consider spending more time doing your homework and less time at the mall, on the phone, playing video games, or on Facebook or other social media.

That is how all great achievers do it. They invest their time on the things that matter to them. They do not quit when confronted with doubts or challenges. Rather, they constantly re-evaluate and revise their purpose, even as they seek help, especially from the "higher" power that resides within. One way to view this *higher* power is to visualize a petite woman who weighs only 140 pounds, but, lifting a 3190-pound Toyota Camry off her seven-year-old son. With no other help in sight, this woman had to draw from a power inside her to save her son from a flipped-over and burning vehicle. When interviewed on television several months later, she said she did not understand how it was possible; all she knew was her burning desire to save her son's life and the willingness to do whatever it took.

When you face a difficult situation, and it feels as if there is no help in sight, I encourage you to reach into that power that resides within. The good news is that like the petite woman, we all have this inner strength that is so much more powerful than we can ever imagine. It is always able and willing to rise up to any occasion with success beyond measure. All that is required on our part is the willingness to seek and receive this divine help. If your purpose for learning seems gigantic and difficult to handle, are you willing to reach in and get help from the power inside of you? You want to answer a definite yes to this question.

6. Will my *purpose for learning* benefit me as well as others?

Know that it will, even if you cannot see it or understand how. The truth about life is this: we are all connected, both through our human creations (Internet, technology, etc.) and through our divine nature (desire for peace, love, success, compassion, etc.). Thus, whatever you do has an impact on others—both far and near. This means that whenever you do well for yourself, it has some benefit for other people as well. Chaos theory—the science of surprise—explains this phenomenon as the butterfly effect. It is the idea that small causes can have large-scale effects. For instance, if you succeed in any aspect of your life, whether it is in education, career, relationships, or business, you are contributing in a positive way to many lives. This starts with those in your immediate vicinity and then radiates outward to those in your community, society, and around the world. How so? Because your success means one additional person making a positive contribution (creating jobs, providing care, mentoring, etc.), and one less person that is jobless, lonely, and without support.

In conclusion, you want to answer yes to all six questions. If you cannot, here is an opportunity to re-examine your *pull to become* and revise your *purpose for learning*. I encourage you to listen to your heart for clarity and guidance. A *purpose for learning* that passes these tests is sure to keep you engaged and motivated so you can achieve your *pull to become* in accelerated time.

CHAPTER 4

THE GAP

Don't be afraid of your fears. They're not there to scare you.
They're there to let you know that something is worth it.

—C. JoyBell

Objectives

- Learners will be able to write a paragraph to explain the meaning of "the gap."
- Learners will be able to determine *the gap* they observe between their current condition and their pull to become, and articulate these gaps using *"I feel challenged by ..."* statements.
- Learners will be able to summarize what they learned about the contents of *the gap*.
- Learners will be able to apply what they learned in this chapter to solve a real-life problem pertaining to *the gap*.

Enduring Understandings

- More often than not, there exists a huge gap between your current condition and your *pull to become*.
- Navigating this gap can be very challenging for a number of reasons: status quo, doubt, procrastination, and fear.

- It is imperative to make decisions from a place of power rather than a place of fear.
- Fear is a constant companion, and befriending it is a great way to ensure you make it less of a hindrance to achieving what you are pulled to become.
- There are two kinds of fear: one is real, the other is imaginary.
- It is always important to test your fear for its veracity.

Essential Questions

- What are gaps?
- What specific gaps do you observe between your current condition and your *pull to become*?
- What did you learn from this chapter about *the gap*?
- How might you apply what you have learned to solve a real-life problem that pertains to gaps in your health, education, career, or relationships?

College and Career Readiness Anchor Standards

- Reading Standards: R.CCR. 1, 2, 3, 4, 7, 8, 9, and 10.
- Writing Standards: W.CCR. 1, 2, 3, 4, 5, 6, 7, 8, 9, and 10.
- Speaking and Listening Standards: SL.CCR.1, 2, 3, 4, 5, and 6.
- Language Standards: L.CCR.1, 2, 3, 4, 5 and 6.

S O FAR, WE have spent time exploring your *identity,* your *pull to become,* and your *purpose for learning.* You have made a decision as to what you would like to *be* and *do.* You have also tested your purpose for learning. It aligns with your *pull to become* as well as with your core values. You know you will grow in knowledge and understanding and that your higher power will help and guide you along the way. Both your *pull to become* and your *purpose for learning* excite you, and best of all, there is plenty of good in it for you as well as for others. With joy and optimism, you have written your purpose-for-learning statement and designed your vision board. If you have not already done so, please do so now! With your purpose statement and vision board in hand, you now have a clearer mental and physical representation of the life you desire to live. You can see it. The more you read your statement and look at your vision board, the more you fall in love with this possible life. You are excited about this possibility for your life. You feel good and full of hope. You are enthusiastic about moving forward with the process of anchoring this *pull to become*—this possibility—and transforming it into your reality.

Yet, as you consider taking the first step, you realize there is a huge difference between your current condition and your *pull to become,* your possible life. This difference is referred to in this book as *the gap.* It could be a gap in your health, education, skill sets, mental attitude, earnings, relationships, etc. There is so much lack and so many obstacles, you might say to yourself. You want to take steps toward your *pull to become,* but the gap seems too wide and deep. It looks dark and ominous! Navigating this gap may be very challenging, for four very important reasons.

First is the gravitational pull of your "comfort zone"—the way things have always been – the status quo. Believe it or not, the status quo does exert a strong pull on unsuspecting individuals. This is because you are familiar and comfortable with the way things have always been. Although you may be unhappy with your current situation, it is non-threatening. You understand it somewhat, and you have been able to manage it well without major crisis. It is now part of you, maybe you have accepted it as your fate, your reality, or your life, and it no longer scares you. "It is what it is," you say to yourself; you can handle it! However, this big *pull to become* is a completely different story. This possibility that you are now considering is beyond your map of reality—totally unfamiliar territory. Perhaps no one in your family has ever contemplated it, much more talked about it. This is scary. The list of unknowns and uncertainties is just too long. You may be wondering whether you really can have this new life that you have imagined for yourself. *"Is it really possible for me and is it what I am truly being pulled to become?"* You ask in self-doubt. With no assuring response, you turn and look around you, and you find that you are all by yourself, standing alone on the edge of a new horizon, a new beginning, in the land of imagination. Perhaps, everyone else you know is standing firmly in the familiar territory, staring at you from a distance and wondering what has come over you. Suddenly, you hear a loud voice from a family member or friend, warning you that you are about to stumble and fall over the edge. This voice of caution overwhelms you. In response, you take one last look at the gap, you hesitate to take a leap, you turn around, and you return to the life you have always known—your familiar and predictable comfort zone.

The second important reason is the feeling of not being "good enough." You look at the beautiful life that you have imagined and decide in your mind that "it is too good or too beautiful for a [fill in the blank] like me." We reel out a long list of mistakes we have made and acting as the judge, we slam the gavel, and pronounce judgement against ourselves: *Not good enough! Doesn't qualify! Not deserving, etc.!* All too often, our minds are so preoccupied with past errors that we fail to recognize what is right about us in the present moment. Unable to let go and forgive ourselves, we engage in self-condemnation and unconsciously disqualify ourselves from having the good that we so much desire. Rather than leaning in, we step aside, stand back, and watch our *pull to become*— our desires, our dreams, and the very things we want—slip away from our grasp.

Nevertheless, remember this truth: we are all humans, and we have all made mistakes—even those who we think are successful and living a dream life. Our sense of "being good enough" is not based on our actions—whether good or bad. It is based on the fact that we have life and that life is fundamentally good. So, if we are breathing, we are deserving of all the good that life has to offer, regardless of past mistakes. We need to remember our true identities and cut loose from the cords of past blunders. We need to deliberately make up our minds that this *pull to become* tugging at our hearts will transform into its physical reality for each of us. We must hold firmly to the belief that if any one person is deserving of a dream life, then everyone (including you and I) is also deserving - no exception!

The third reason is procrastination – also known as the thief of time. Procrastination is the habit of putting off something that requires immediate attention. A twenty-year-old woman whom I had worked with when she was in her teens had this confession to make when we ran into each other several years later. "When I was with you, I was fired up, tuned in, and focused on achieving my goals. So, I did all my journal entries, reflection questions, etc. I was up to date on all my lessons. I was committed, and I actually read some chapters multiple times. Then Easter came, and school was out. I went to spend some time with my cousins out of state. Things happened, and procrastination set in. A week passed, then it became four weeks and then four months, and before I knew it, other things overshadowed the plans I had made for achieving my goals. My *pull to become* got obscured. A year or two later, I had done nothing. And here I am, face to face with you, embarrassed that I let procrastination get between me and my dreams."

This young woman's experience is a very common one. Anyone can procrastinate, even the most disciplined of us. Do not beat yourself up for slacking off a little. Nevertheless, watch out! Procrastination is sneaky. It will creep up on you and attempt to shift your attention elsewhere. So, if you are having difficulty managing your time wisely, seek help. There are many resources available to you. Search the Internet, local library, YouTube videos, Technology Entertainment Design (TED) talks, etc. You could even speak with your school counselors, mentors, or coaches, and share your concerns with them. They will be glad to give you valuable advice, help you stay focused, and hold you accountable as necessary.

The last and perhaps the biggest challenge is fear. Fear is the source of most of the challenges you are likely to encounter in *the gap*, and it is likely to remain a constant companion throughout your journey. It is the voice in your head which tries to convince you that failure is inevitable. All sorts of fears—including fear of ridicule, fear of isolation, or even fear of success—will tag along, attempting to slow you down or stop you from moving forward. No wonder many people consider fear the root cause of all failures. Be aware, though, that fear can also be the springboard from which you launch yourself over and beyond the gap. In essence, fear can be a foe or a friend.

As a foe, fear will fill you with self-doubt, confusion, worry, and anxiety. It will control, cripple, or even stop you in your tracks if you allow it. You may feel so overwhelmed by fear that you choose lower, and abandon your desire to *be*, and choose higher. In my experience, there is no worse enemy of the *pull to become* a bigger, smarter, and better version of one's self than fear. When besieged by fear, you may feel chained to the past, oblivious to the present, and anxious about your future. Fear weakens you and erodes the willingness to navigate the gap. Fear causes you to over-think or over-analyze the situation to the point that a decision or action is never taken - in effect paralyzing the dream. No wonder fear is often viewed as a malignant, disempowering companion.

There is a Cherokee fable about a young man who goes to the chief of his village for help because he is filled with fear. He has come of age, and as is customary, it is time for him to go out on his vision quest. However, he is gripped by fear! He is fearful because he is going to have to leave the familiar and safe village community. He will have to leave the family compound and go out alone into the jungle where there are many wild and dangerous animals: tigers, lions, and hyenas, etc. He is very frightened of the jungle beasts—they might attack and eat him alive! So, he goes to the village chief and he says, "I want to do the vision quest, but I am afraid and confused. It feels as if there is a battle going on inside of me. It's like two coyotes fighting. One says I can succeed on this quest and the other one says I cannot succeed. It is a fierce battle, chief; they are both very strong coyotes! And as the fight continues, I'm even more frightened and confused, not knowing whether to undertake this vision quest or abandon it altogether. Chief, I need your wisdom and guidance."

The chief compassionately counsels the young man to pitch his tent in favor of the one that says he will succeed. Puzzled, the young man asked the chief how he could be so sure about that. The chief replied, "Because that is the one you will feed with your attention."

This story is a powerful reminder that fear can be a menacing and treacherous companion. When faced with a decision, many people tend to cling to the familiar out of fear. Like the young Native American man, we are often confused and crippled by fear. In so doing, we may miss out on the very thing that will bring us success, peace and happiness. In my opinion, by far too many of us live our lives as if chained to the familiar. Consequently, we often overlook options and erroneously dismiss possibilities due to fear. What we must recognize is that fear and freedom cannot co-exist for long – one must prevail. Which one will you allow to dominate your thinking, choices, actions, and life?

As you ponder the above question, also consider this proposition: fear could also be an ally – make pact with it – befriend your fear! If you make fear a friend, this relationship can lead to freedom, and ultimately to power, success and happiness. Consider, for example, the case of a colleague of mine who shared with me how she had befriended fear to her advantage. According to her, when she was a very young teacher she had been terrified of public speaking. Facilitating instruction in the classroom had never been a problem.

However, when it came to speaking in front of audiences outside the classroom, she became, as she described it, a "nervous wreck." Not only did she freeze physically, she got a mental freeze as well. In an instant, she would forget what to say, her stomach would start to churn, there would be a lump in her throat, and she would sweat profusely. This intense physical and mental reaction to public speaking was stifling her career growth until she decided to befriend fear. She did so by joining Toastmasters, where week after week she stood before supportive audiences and delivered speeches. These were impromptu table topics as well as prepared speeches, and she gave these speeches regardless of fear. She recalled that after several months, one day, in the middle of a speech, she turned and looked around, but fear was nowhere to be found. She saw only a room full of applauding audience. That was the death of her fear of public speaking. "Since then," she concluded, "fear has never been able to cripple me. Although still a constant companion, it no longer controls my actions. Ironically, it sometimes serves as the motivation to set and achieve some of my big personal and career goals."

What is fear, really, and where does it come from? Experts describe fear as a painful emotion triggered by both external and internal experiences. They contend that there are two types of fear: real or imagined. For example, if you come face to face with a wild animal, say a tiger, you may be gripped by fear, an emotion of anxiety and paralysis. This fear is real, and most people will react in a similar way when terrified by the imminent danger in front of them. So, we see that real fear is triggered by external factors. The other type of fear is triggered by internal factors with no visible external causes, only invisible thought forms. They are figments of the imagination, thoughts in your mind generated from inside of you. These fears are simply not real.

And here is the good news! Most of the fears occupying the gap between you and the desires of your heart are not real. They are merely a state of mind. They are illusions created by your very own imagination. If you are willing to accept that you created them inside of you, then, you can *un-create* them just as easily. How? Again, through your vivid imagination. Know that you can exercise your free will to redirect your mind away from the fear thoughts that is keeping you separated from your *pull to become* a bigger, better, smarter, and more successful you. You can invalidate the fear in *the gap.*

How much fear will you allow to stand between you and your *pull to become?* Keep in mind that everyone experiences fear at one time or another and that no one is immune to fear. Hence, you have to learn to interact with fear in a bold way, by first acknowledging its presence and then moving right ahead with your plans. Do not let fear get in your way.

To step into your gap even in the face of fear, I invite you to put your fear to the test with these five questions:

1. Is this fear real or imagined? What are the facts?
2. What is this fear trying to protect me from?
3. Does this fear require my attention right now? If so, what can I do about it right now?
4. What is the next step, and who can I call for help?
5. What is the worst or the best that can happen? Then what?

Be mindful as you explore these questions. Dig in as deeply as necessary with each question. But remember your true identity—a divine being having a human experience. Know that in this journey toward your *pull to become* you will be okay, no matter what happens. You can have the desires of your heart if you want it bad enough and are willing to do what it takes. Acknowledge your fear, accept it, and take the necessary action that is immediately possible. In the meantime, release yourself from the chains of the past, and appreciate the now – your present moment. This is where your power to face and overcome fear resides. Honor this moment with gratitude, thanksgiving, and a "possibility mindset." In addition, remember that you are extremely adaptable and strong. Others have navigated this gap and achieved stupendous success. So can you! Remember, you are *No Less than Genius.*

PART II

✦✦✦✦✦

EMPOWERMENT

The power to change your life lies in the simplest of steps.
—Steve Maraboli

WELCOME TO THE second phase of our journey together, and congratulations for your persistence! In the preceding chapter, you came face to face with *the gap*—that difference between your current reality and your *pull to become*. You have tried to look beyond the fear looming in this gap, but perhaps you are unable to do so. You are terrified! You think about the monstrous creatures that may be lurking in this deep, wide, and ominous gap. You imagine that they are waiting and ready to devour you if you dare step out of your comfort zone and into the gap. At the same time, you have the picture of your *pull to become* vividly etched in your mind. You see a brighter future ahead of you, something magnificent and wonderful. You sense that this desire could become your reality, and you are hopeful and joyful. Your heart skips a beat; you are excited about living this beautiful life that you have imagined! Yet, you are still afraid, concerned and hesitant about taking the next step forward. Regardless, your desire for this *pull to become* remains strong—you want to achieve it and live it! You are aware that the road is narrow, steep, and full of uncertainties. You realize this could be a long and lonesome journey. You might have to give up things, to leave some familiar habits, attitudes, friends, and even family members behind. You realize you are taking a risk – there are no guarantees – but you also know that this is a risk that is well worth taking. You are willing to step out in faith and take a chance for the brighter future you are imagining. You have come this far, and you realize there is no turning back now.

Consequently, kindly allow me to introduce you to another companion on this journey. Everybody knows a farmer's tools are his ever-present companion - he does not go to farm without his tools. Just like the farmer, you will need to take with you some tools of empowerment on your journey. One of them is hidden in this popular riddle written for the benefit of mankind by a "good Samaritan," – author yet unknown. See if you can recognize it.

I am your constant companion.

I am your greatest helper or your heaviest burden.

I will push you onward or drag you down to failure. I am completely at your command.

Half the things you do you might just as well turn over to me; I will be able to do them quickly and correctly if you just give me guidance.

I am easily managed, but you must be firm with me.

Show me exactly what you want done, what you want created, and I will work on it automatically.

I am the servant of all great men and women;

But, alas, I am also that which brings failure to them. Those who are great I have made great.

Those who are failures I have made failures.

I am not a machine, but I work with the precision of a fine machine plus the intelligence of the smartest person you know.

You may run me for profit, or you may run me to ruin; it makes no difference to me.

Take me. Train me.

Be firm with me, and I will place the world at your feet.

Be easy with me, casual with me, convenient with me, and I will destroy every dream you have.

WHO AM I?

~ Anonymous

You guessed right—I am your thoughts!

Thoughts are powerful. And as the riddle pointed out, they can make or break you. They go with you everywhere, and they give form to your experiences. For example, if you think empowering thoughts, you feel strong and capable. On the other hand, if you think disempowering thoughts, you feel weak and incapable. This is what is meant by the mind and body connection. The idea that the thoughts in your mind can produce physical sensations in your body. Remember the teacher who was afraid of public speaking and her physical reactions? You know mind-body connection is real when you develop goose bumps simply by thinking about an empathetic situation, or you begin to sweat profusely when you are placed on the "hot seat" – with no word spoken yet! Some people even develop instant headaches or stomach cramps just by thinking of taking a test or faced with a situation they feel unprepared for. There are many stories about people who overcame terminal illness and grim diagnosis and went on to experience full recovery and subsequently great health the moment they understood the power of their thoughts and its relationship to their physical experience.

Therefore, if this idea of mind–body connection still sounds airy-fairy to you, feel free to explore it further. There is a large body of scientific research that supports it - the idea that your thoughts have the power to create your physical experiences. In other words, you become what you think about. To know that the (formless) thoughts you hold in your mind create what you experience in your physical (form) world is very empowering—because it validates the notion that your life experience is malleable to your thinking. To put it another way, this means that you can change your experience of life by simply changing your thoughts about your experiences. For example, if you think you are tired, hungry, not loveable or not smart, etc. these thoughts will set in motion corresponding energies that match them, and you instantly begin to experience fatigue, hunger, not loveable and not smart. What is the lesson to be learned here? It is simply that you are the master of your life, the captain of your ship, and that you can stir your life in any direction you want by simply shifting your thoughts in that direction. Fear thoughts produce fear, and power thoughts generate power. As the riddle indicated, we all have the power of choice - the option to choose the thoughts we will take as constant companions on the journey to our *pull to become.*

CHAPTER 5

PRODUCTIVE AND AFFIRMATIVE THINKING

Instead of worrying about what you cannot control,
shift your energy to what you can create.

—Roy T. Bennett

Objectives

- Learners will be able to write a three-paragraph essay to explain their understanding of productive and affirmative thinking.
- Learners will be able to analyze each of the seven genius-level thinking strategies, and explain how they will apply each of these seven strategies to generate ideas for overcoming specific challenges.
- Learners will be able to write a paragraph to summarize what they learned in this chapter.
- Learners will be able to apply what they have learned to solve a real- life problem.

Enduring Understandings

- Productive thinking promotes flexibility of thought that supports multiple perspectives to problem solving.
- Affirmative thinking is a mental and emotional attitude that looks on the brighter side of life.

- Thought is energy, and the energy generated by thought is creative.
- Productive and affirmative thoughts can convert potential energy into a usable form for achieving your *pull to become.*
- Your body responds to your thoughts: productive and affirming thoughts strengthen the muscles.
- The thoughts you hold in mind produce your experiences.
- If you master your thoughts, you master every aspect of your life.

Essential Questions

- What is productive and affirmative thinking?
- How will you apply each of the seven genius-level thinking strategies to generate ideas for overcoming specific challenges?
- What have you learned in this chapter?
- How might you apply what you have learned to solve a real-life problem?

College and Career Readiness Anchor Standards

- Reading Standards: R.CCR. 1, 2, 3, 4, 7, 8, 9, and 10.
- Writing Standards: W.CCR. 1, 2, 3, 4, 5, 6, 7, 8, 9, and 10.
- Speaking and Listening Standards: SL.CCR.1, 2, 3, 4, 5, and 6.
- Language Standards: L.CCR.1, 2, 3, 4, 5 and 6.

I N THIS CHAPTER, your thinking is showing up again as a companion on your journey. This time though, it is filled with options, not with fear. Therefore, when you are confronted with a problem, you not only apply your prior knowledge, but also expand your thinking to generate multiple options and fresh perspectives to solving it. This is the essence of productive thinking. For example, instead of simply asking, "What have I learned in my past to solve a problem?" Applying productive way of thinking will enable you expand your thinking and ask, "In how many different ways can I view this problem?" "How might I reframe this problem and generate multiple options that I can apply to solving this problem?" Asking these or similar questions help you produce many ideas for solving the problem. This is *genius*! As a genius, you think productively and not only reproductively. This means that when faced with challenges, you do more than simply reproduce and reapply what worked in the past; you also explore many different ways to tackle the problem. Assume for instance, that you are trying to explain the concept of fifteen to a second grader. You can apply productive thinking to generate 10 + 5; 3 groups of 5; 14 + 1; 20 - 5; etc. The idea is that you seek to generate many alternatives to solving a problem. You explore and consider the least as well as the most likely strategies. Productive thinking sheds new light on issues. Thus, utilizing it can be refreshing and energizing.

You will also need to utilize affirmative thinking—a positive outlook to life. Affirmative thinking is beneficial because it is optimistic, and expects desired results despite the temptation to think otherwise. The good news is that together, both types of thinking arise from the core belief that life is fundamentally good and that there is a genius mind present in you. An even better news is that you have free access to this genius mind. It is available for your use in any place, time, or situation. Your genius mindset is always present, it is productive and affirming, and you can use it to generate ideas that will validate you, and also help you create anything you desire.

Keep in mind that all thought is energy, and energy is creative. Therefore, all your thoughts are creative. In other words, thoughts are the unseen background energy that creates everything you experience, as well as things you can see and touch. Remember the riddle at the beginning of the section? Through it, we learned that everything created and experienced, first began as a thought. In essence, the thoughts we hold in our minds create our experiences. Since all thought is energy, then it implies that fear thoughts, as well as productive and affirmative thoughts are energy too. However, the difference in experience is that they occupy different energy levels. Imagine a totem pole. Whereas fear and other disempowering thoughts occupy the lower levels; productive, affirmative, and other empowering thoughts occupy the higher end of the pole. Fear thoughts produce low energy, constriction, and containment; there is not enough energy to create what you want at this low energy level. On the other hand, productive and affirmative thoughts generate the high energy that is able to support your growth, creativity, and expansion. Therefore, it is imperative that you become conscious of your energy level at all times by way of your thinking. This is because all the energy you need to achieve your *pull to become* is available only at the higher, and not the lower levels of thought.

Among the many scientific research that demonstrate the empowering or disempowering attributes of thought is the work of David Hawkins. He built upon the findings of his predecessor, Dr. Diamond, who first demonstrated that a muscle goes instantly weak or strong in response to the energy level of the dominating thought. In other words, if you hold negative thoughts in your mind, your body loses energy, and your muscles go weak. Conversely, positive thoughts produce energy that instantly strengthens your muscles. Dr. Hawkins went on to develop a scale to calibrate the relative power of energy generated by different thoughts. He did so through a modified version of his predecessor's simple muscle-testing technique. The test begins with two people, one of whom acts as the subject. The subject closes his or her eyes and stretches out one arm sideways, keeping it parallel to the ground. He or she thinks of a true statement and holds this thought in mind. The second person presses down on the wrist of the subject's extended arm and says, "Resist." That is all there is to the test! After tens of thousands of clinical tests, the results are said to be consistent—false or negative thoughts weakened the subjects' muscles, and they could not resist the pressure. On the other hand, truth and affirming thoughts strengthened the subjects' muscles, and they were able to withstand the pressure on the wrist. The table below is an excerpt and adaptation of these energy levels calibrated by David Hawkins. He termed it the Map of Consciousness (Hawkins, 2002).

Life-View or Perspective about Life	Associated Thoughts	Energy Level	Associated Emotions
Meaningful	Reason	400	Understanding
Hopeful	Willingness	310	Optimism
Feasible	Courage	200	Affirmation
Frightening	Fear	100	Anxiety
Miserable	Shame	20	Humiliation

A review of the complete map of consciousness shows a scale of 20 to 1000. David Hawkins further explained that if you think about great people like Gandhi, Mother Teresa, or Abraham Lincoln, these thoughts calibrate at over 700, which invokes positive feelings that energize you, but thoughts of people like Adolph Hitler will instantly generate negative feelings that weaken you. I find this experiment fascinating, and if you are like me, you may consider trying it out yourself. There are some precautions, though: no jewelry on the outstretched arm, no glasses or hats. Hawkins's work is a reminder for us to be aware of the energy level from which we are operating at any moment in time. To create the results you want, practice operating from productive and affirming thoughts that carry high energy.

As we have learned, everything in our physical world was first an unseen and formless energy (thought) before it was transmuted into physical things that are seen and tangible. For example, remember that the book you are reading right now was first a thought in the mind of the author, who then took appropriate action steps (chose the subject, wrote the manuscript, submitted for publication, etc.) before it materialized into its physical equivalent. So it is with the chairs and tables in your classroom, lecture halls, and office as well as with your clothes, the shoes you are wearing, etc. Everything created was first a thought that was converted to its physical equivalent through deliberate action steps taken by people just like you and me. Understanding and applying this basic truth holds the key to your success. The awareness that you have the capacity to create your heart's desire in every aspect of your life by simply swapping fear thoughts for productive and affirmative thoughts, and then following up with appropriate action is empowering.

Napoleon Hill summed up the creative power of thoughts in these words:

"Each thought creates its kind,
And they speed over the track to bring you back
Whatever went out from your mind."

I encourage you to reflect on these words and allow them to remind you that you are what you think. The thoughts you hold in your mind mimic your experiences in the physical world. If you hold productive and affirmative thoughts, these thoughts will generate the energy to bring back to you creativity and validation. Over time, you will begin to experience yourself as a bigger and better version of yourself. Productive and affirmative thoughts will propel you forward, regardless of the magnetic pull of the past. You must understand that you have the ability to move past fear and shift your thoughts in the direction of your *pull to become*. To change your life experiences, you simply have to shift your thinking from what you do not want to what you do want. All the successful people you know, and perhaps those you secretly envy, understand and practice this truth in their everyday lives. They have had to make a shift to productive and affirmative thinking before they achieved their *pull to become*, especially when faced with the fear of the gap.

Accordingly, I encourage you to master your thinking and master every aspect of your life. Know that there cannot be a problem without a solution. There cannot be a *pull to become* without a path to achieving it. Even when you come up against big obstacles and you are stuck in the gap, you must recognize that there is a way forward. This may not be immediately visible to you, but if you use your productive thinking to affirm the presence of a solution, this thinking will magnetize the solution, and it will show up somehow. Thus, you must learn to release from your mind any thought that isn't the image of exactly what you are seeking, and you must place your thought and attention on everything that is the image of what you desire.

Equally important, be reminded that within every one of us is an infinite power for good that is far greater than we can ever imagine! This power is only potential power. With productive and affirmative thinking, we can convert this potential power into a usable energy form that we can then apply to creating anything we desire. Be aware of this for sure: practicing productive and affirmative thinking will increase your knowledge of, and interaction with this power within, which will in turn generate an upsurge in your creative capacities.

All that is required of you is a modest willingness to open your mind to the possibility of a brighter future. Know that it is okay to admit that "In my present circumstance, I don't know what to believe about what's possible for me, but I am open to the idea." That is exactly what I am asking from you right now— a simple willingness to open up to the possibility that you can transform your *pull to become* into its tangible form with productive and affirmative thinking. The energy of productive and affirmative thinking have changed many lives, and so it will do for many more, including you, me, and everyone else who chooses to practice this type of thinking on a daily basis.

The next few paragraphs will highlight some strategies for generating productive and affirmative thinking. Be reminded once again that both types of thinking take you beyond fear and limitations, and into the territory of options and possibilities. They are ways of taking the low-energy fear thoughts and converting them into the higher energy levels where all answers, solutions, insights, inspiration, enthusiasm, and creativity reside. Below are seven genius-level thinking strategies that scholars like Michael Michalko (2011) suggest you can utilize to enable you to achieve your *pull to become*, regardless of your challenges.

Consider alternatives. Realizing that you are *No Less than Genius*, you must allow the genius in you to reveal itself by consciously seeking alternative means of solving old or new problems. This means seeking multiple perspectives that are fresh and innovative and applying them to the issue at hand. Wayne Dyer said it eloquently in these few words: "You cannot solve a problem with the same mindset that created it." This implies that in order to solve a problem you must be willing to view that problem from many unbiased perspectives, while affirming that there is an answer to the problem, which currently resides beyond your usual way of viewing the problem.

Sketch your thought. This means give your thought a visible form by writing your thoughts down. You may also represent them as diagrams, maps, graphs, charts, drawings, vision boards, pictures or shapes that depict relationships, etc. The ability to do this is essential because as experts say, our minds think and see in pictures. Einstein once noted that not all thoughts can be represented clearly in spoken words. Thus, writing your thoughts down help to clarify your thinking and etches your *pull to become* vividly in your mind while simultaneously ensuring that it remains a priority for you. Keeping your thoughts in visible form is a powerful means of recognizing what you want when you see it. It is also an effective way of reminding yourself that every good thing you see in life is possible for you, because it is simply the thought of someone who cared enough to give it a visible form.

Formulate unique combinations. The idea here is to produce something new and fresh by weaving together solitary ideas. Dean Simonton's 1989 book *Scientific Genius* suggests that making novel combinations is a characteristic that sets geniuses apart. Einstein, for example, was able to formulate the concept of mass-energy equivalence, as expressed in his famous equation E=mc2. He did so by combining the separate ideas of energy, mass, and the speed of light, even though he did not invent any one of these three concepts. In recognition of his genius, Michael Michalko remarked that Einstein "was able to look at the same world as everyone else and see something different." Although you may be currently reluctant to view yourself as a genius, understand that you have the same ability to create brand new things or solve problems by combining existing dissimilar ideas or improving them. The same infinite intelligence that was available to all the geniuses of old still exist. It has never been denied anyone, and never will. It is available for you to use so that you can demonstrate the genius in you by creating the life of your dreams.

I encourage you to use your thinking to affirm that you are inseparable from this boundless intelligence within you. It is never absent. You are like it. In fact, you are it, and so were the geniuses of old. Accordingly, whenever you are confronted with a problem or challenge, remind yourself of this ever-present intelligence within you. Affirm it with your thinking, and believe that you deserve everything good that life has to offer. This is where you utilize *I am* statements. Say to yourself, *"Life is good, and so I am. Life is generous, and so I am. Life is creative, and so I am,"* etc. I encourage you to continue reminding yourself of this unison with universal intelligence until you feel a shift in your thinking. The more often you practice thinking productively and affirmatively, the quicker and more available your desired experience will be. You will move to a higher energy level where there is no gap between you and your *pull to become* and *do*. All the answers you need will be right there at this energy level. All solutions, guidance, and support will also be available at this energy level, where everything is possible. So, no matter what the situation may be, you can uplift yourself with productive and affirmative thinking, using the spoken *"I am ..."* statements.

Make Connections. Geniuses have the uncanny ability to establish meaningful associations between dissimilar things. In his research paper *A Theory about Genius*, Michael Michalko reports a plethora of evidence depicting this genius quality as exhibited by the following:

- Leonardo da Vinci, who observed a correlation between the dissimilar sound of a bell and a stone hitting water. This association enabled him to successfully make the argument that sound travels in waves.
- Nikola Tesla drew a link between the setting sun and a motor. He made the AC motor possible by having the "motor's magnetic field rotate inside the motor, similar to the way that the sun rotates (Michalko, 2016). If interested, you may read more about Michael Michalko's work at http://creativethinking. net/a-theory-about genius/#sthash.8rPLOUXg.dpbs.

Take a look at your experiences, your education, your skills and talents. Do they appear disjointed at this time? Apply the genius mindset that resides in you to forge a meaningful connection. This may increase your awareness of possibilities that could serve as the solution to your most pressing challenges. For instance, recalling and merging my experience of life's highs and lows led me to my purpose in life. This is possible for you too, simply because you share this genius mindset with all of humanity. Therefore, whenever faced with difficult challenges that seem to be coming at you from different directions, use your genius mindset to establish relationships between your disparate experiences. Realize that there is a gift hidden in every pain, disappointment or "failure." Honor this unseen gift, and affirm the solution to the problem. Over time, this affirmation will become your way of thinking—a realization that dissolves all notions of impossibility, which will in turn engender the can-be and can-do mindset that inspires extraordinary achievements.

Be Creative. Geniuses are highly creative! The life that you have is a creative genius. It is forever seeking a bigger and more robust demonstration of itself in, through, and as you. In essence, you are a creative genius by nature. Your *pull to become* and *purpose for learning* will keep you engaged, motivated, and guide you toward what you are to create and produce. As a genius, you will create things beyond your wildest imagination. So, let your genius shine— create in spite of obstacles. You don't have to create it perfectly all the time. History has it that Einstein wrote and published over 248 papers, but he is best known for his one paper on *relativity*. Again, recorded history has it that Thomas Edison, who held the patent to almost 1100 inventions, set a personal quota of creating a minor invention every ten days and one major invention every six months. In fact, after studying over two thousand famous scientists, Dean Simonton, of the University of California in Davis, concluded that renowned scholars characteristically produce massive works year after year—some great and others mediocre— but they produce enormously, regardless. Typically, out of this huge quantity come the one or two pieces of quality work for which they receive accolades and professional recognition. So be yourself— create! Although you may not know the detail right now, affirm that it is being worked out in your favor – get started.

Tolerate ambivalence. Geniuses are not frustrated by contradictions or uncertainties. Rather, they exercise the ability to think and manage different and opposing thoughts simultaneously. Michalko points out that the notable researcher Dr. Albert Rothenberg saw this quality in many geniuses including, Mozart, Picasso, etc. The idea here is that holding opposites together suspends limiting thoughts—a condition that generates the free flow of creative juices in all of us. This is the belief that enabled the physicist Niels Bohr to conceptualize light as both a particle and a wave. But how can you conceive of the fear in your gap as both a foe and a friend? It's simple—just think like the genius that you are, and affirm that the notion "opposites attract" will work in your favor.

Expect the unexpected. Lastly, geniuses prepare themselves for unintended discoveries. To do this, set out in pursuit of your *pull to become*. You may do all the "right" things, befriend your fear, think productively and affirmatively, but nothing seems to be working for you. You may stumble and fall, and perhaps you think you have failed. Take heart and know that this experience is common to all, even the geniuses and the most successful people you admire. Rather than accept failure as the end, geniuses view it as a new beginning— an opportunity to be redirected to something bigger and better. In some sense, this "creative accident" is a blessing in disguise, one that holds the insight for a higher order of creativity. Consequently, I encourage you to let go of the feeling of disappointment, worry, or ridicule that may be associated with failed attempts at your *pull to become*. Exhale and relax, knowing that every challenge or disappointment bears with it an equivalent seed of opportunity. This is the time to apply productive and affirmative thinking to the perceived failure. You need to let go, and as you do so, you will open up to new creative ideas.

I invite you to practice these seven strategies for productive thinking on a regular basis. They are very useful and powerful exercises that can help you generate ideas for more creativity in school, work, or life itself. Note however, that their power can only be unleashed through daily practice. You can do it just about anywhere—in line at the library, bus stop, grocery store, in the shower or classroom—and as often as you can. An immediate benefit is that it keeps your energy level high. The higher your energy level, the more creative energy you have available for transforming your *pull to become* into your reality. Remember, only high energy creates what you want. Low energy, although also creative, creates things you do not want. Note that the power to create or to destroy resides within your thinking. So, whether you think you can or think you can't, this power will go to work to make sure you are right. Here is the lesson in this: it is possible to cause the very law that restricted you in the past to bring you freedom now. How? By simply changing how you think, and what you think about.

For forty years, John Maxwell studied a diverse population of successful people, and here is the commonality he found: the way they think! Maxwell goes on to add that the way we think is the single most important thing that separates successful people from unsuccessful ones. According to Maxwell, one of the unique ways that successful people reason is that they embrace possibility—the notion that there is always a way, a solution, an answer, even if it is not immediately visible. Successful people look for and affirm the good in every situation, no matter how grim. They think they can achieve their *pull to become*, and they do because they practice productive and affirmative thinking.

I'd like to close this section by leaving you with some helpful quotes to keep in mind.

1. The only place where your dream becomes impossible is in your own thinking.

   —Robert Schuller

2. Our thoughts determine our destiny. Our destiny determines our legacy.

   —John C. Maxwell

3. Everything is created twice, first in thought and then in form.

   —Mary Manin Morrissey

4. Life consists of what a man is thinking about all day.

    —Ralph Waldo Emerson

5. You are today where your thoughts have brought you. You will be tomorrow where your thoughts take you.

    —James Allen

6. The sum total of all our thoughts is either silently attracting good to us or repelling it from us.

    —Ernest Holmes

7. Change your thoughts, change your life.

    —Wayne Dyer

8. Never underestimate the power of thought; it is the greatest path to discovery.

    —Idowu Koyenikan

9. You attract to you the predominant thoughts that you're holding in your awareness, whether those thoughts are conscious or unconscious. That's the rub.

    — Michael Bernard Beckwith

10. My thoughts run all my errands, getting me everything I want consciously or unconsciously.

    —Helen Mozia

CHAPTER 6

SUPPORT TEAM

Sticks in a bundle are unbreakable.

—Kenyan proverb

Objectives

- Learners will be able to write two paragraphs explaining the meaning of a support team as well as the importance of having one.
- Learners will be able to verbally communicate what they learned about the composition, qualities, and agreements made by support teams.
- Learners will be able to create a support team for their *pull to become* in the four domains of health, education, career, and relationships.
- Learners will be able to describe in writing, the qualities that each member of their support team will contribute, as well as what they are personally willing to give in return.
- Learners will be able to apply what they have learned in this chapter to help a friend create a support team.

Enduring Understandings

- No one succeeds alone.
- Everyone needs a support team.

- A support team gives access to knowledge and information that is not available when working alone.
- The people you surround yourself with affect your level of success.
- You are very likely to succeed in life if the people around you refuse to let you fail.
- It is important to build agreements with your support team regarding how this partnership will operate.

Essential Questions

- What is a support team? Why is it important to have a support team?
- How will you verbally communicate what you have learned about the composition, qualities, and agreements made by support teams to a friend?
- Who will you ask to be members of your support team in the domains of health, education, career and relationships?
- How will you describe and analyze the qualities that each member of your support team will contribute, as well as what you are personally willing to give in return?
- How might you apply what you have learned in this chapter to help a friend create a support team for his/her dream?

College and Career Readiness Anchor Standards

- Reading Standards: R.CCR. 1, 2, 3, 4, 7, 8, 9, and 10.
- Writing Standards: W.CCR. 1, 2, 3, 4, 5, 6, 7, 8, 9, and 10.
- Speaking and Listening Standards: SL.CCR.1, 2, 3, 4, 5, and 6.
- Language Standards: L.CCR.1, 2, 3, 4, 5 and 6.

ANOTHER EMPOWERING TOOL for your quest is a support team. A support team is a group of people, perhaps two or more, who believe in you and are willing to come together with the intention to support your *pull to become*. Imagine that you are driving to an important event. On the way, you notice your gas tank is almost empty, so you stop at a gas station to refuel. After the fill-up, you enter your car, turn on the ignition, the car stalls, and then it dies. It will not restart. Multiple attempts to restart your car fail. Then you discover the culprit—the battery. It is dead; it needs a boost. So, you call for roadside assistance, and they jump-start your battery with a cable connected to a greater power source. Within a few minutes, your battery is reenergized, your car starts, you step in, drive off, and continue your journey knowing that roadside assistance is always only a phone call away.

So it is with this journey toward your *pull to become*. You are going to need help along the way, because no one succeeds alone. Ken Blanchard said it beautifully: "None of us is as smart as all of us." We all need the help and cooperation of others to achieve our goals. Napoleon Hill established this truth in the 1930s, when he was commissioned by Andrew Carnegie to study successful people. Among other things, Hill discovered that successful people create a support team—a group of people whose intention is to help each other achieve their goals. With this collective support, each member of the team achieves more, and do so, much faster than if they were working alone. According to Hill, this accelerated success occurs because consulting, and working harmoniously with others, generate a higher mind that is more intelligent than the mind of any individual in the group. Hill called this higher mind the mastermind—a higher, smarter mind that becomes available for the use of each member of the team to solve problems and achieve goals more efficiently.

The implication of Hill's discovery is far-reaching. Not only do we need a mastermind or support team, but also, we need to be mindful that the people we surround ourselves with matter. Just like the mastermind group, these people have everything to do with our level of success.

How so? Because of what you already know - birds of the same feather flock together. We all tend to view life, think, and act like the people we call our friends. Thus, if you hang around success-conscious people, you are bound to engage in actions that breed success. However, if you surround yourself with failure-conscious people, you are also more likely to engage in activities that will bring you failure. Are you a high school or college graduate? If so, notice that most of your friends are graduates as well. If you are not, also notice that the majority of your friends are not graduates either. The lesson here is that either you can choose to surround yourself with people who uplift and inspire you, or you can choose to spend time with people who ridicule you for thinking differently and aiming high. On this journey, the people you want on your side are those who will support you to *be* and *do* more with your life. These people will not judge you. Rather, they will affirm you and your ability to achieve what you are pulled to become and do.

Support teams are empowering, so you would be wise to create and take one with you along this journey. Then, whenever you feel depleted—your power is waning and energy is running low, or you feel stuck, not knowing what to do or how to take the next step forward—you can turn to your support team for guidance. A support team is powerful in that they will never let you fail. Working closely with them will engender an invisible, intangible larger mind field that is smarter than the mind of any individual member of the team. Through collaboration with your support team, you will gain access to the larger mind field that has abundant ideas and information to get you unstuck. Your support team will hold you at a higher energy level, bring you fresh insights and perspectives that actually will help you see options you may have closed off. When you feel doubtful, your support team will help to redirect your thinking and help you remember the creative genius within you.

A support team will provide guidance that enables you to

experience yourself as a much bigger and capable person. Your support team will always be available to remind you that your *pull to become* is possible, and that there is not a single thing you could think of doing that you cannot achieve. They will stand with you and encourage you. They will help you remember what is true for, and about you. Bear in mind that it is usually easier for somebody else to see your brilliance than it is for you to see it yourself. Therefore, your support team will magnify the genius that is within you and will remind you of the power that is already at work to overcome any perceived obstacle.

Your support team believes in possibilities. They will offer the support and structure that you need to achieve what you are being pulled to become. This will be high level of support, much like the amplified energy generated by a group of batteries as opposed to the limited energy generated by a single battery. So, reflect on this question for a moment: What would be possible for you if the people around you refused to let you fail? Without a support team, you will find yourself constricted at times by your own limiting thinking. Members of your support team will help you expand your thinking. Your support team will act as your partners and will help you generate a higher power of believing that you can tap into for insight and inspiration. For these reasons, creating and maintaining a support team is an absolute necessity on this journey.

Who are you going to ask to be members of your support team? If you have a support team already, then perhaps it is time to deepen your commitment to each other's success. Personally, I do have a support team for my *pull to become*. I am also part of the support team for others. Sometimes we meet face to face or by phone. For many years I have had a 7:00 a.m. Saturday walk with a friend of mine who is a member of my support team. Like me, she holds high potential; she's seeking to create things to benefit her community, and she supports me in creating my desires. During those times when I am feeling discouraged, she is there to remember and remind me what's true about me, my potential, and my unlimited possibilities. From another friend, I'll get a phone call about four times a month, and he'll say: "I am calling to check up on you and wondering how your project is going." He'll say something that encourages and empowers me. I also give encouragement and support back to members of my team. I find this exchange very rewarding, because as I give back, my mind expands with new and brighter ideas. Having a support team is very important to your success, but you have to want it, and then you have to create one that is right for you.

If you do not already have one, here are some suggestions for creating a support team to help you navigate the gap between your current condition and your *pull to become* and *do*.

First, and foremost, identify people you respect. Endeavor to form a close-knit group of individuals whom you respect, and who are willing to lift you up when you are down. Remember, we learn a lot from those we admire and respect. We may even pick up their behaviors. So, if you're concerned about your own ability in a certain area, find people who are good at it. Pay attention to what they do and how they do it.

Second, seek advice from those who have been there before—they give great advice, and they also know how to push you to be the best version of yourself. Do you know someone who is successfully doing what you'd like to do? Arrange to meet with that person. Seek his or her ideas and perspectives as you traverse the gap.

Third, you may also take inspiration from people you've never met who are doing good things in the world. Sometimes a great support team can come from an unexpected place. Be open! Read biographies and leadership books; watch Ted Talks—whatever works for you and helps you grow.

Finally, you want somebody who you know has your best interests at heart, someone who will stand by you through challenges and remind you that there cannot be any problem without a solution. Sometimes you don't even know you are trapped in limited thinking because you have come to believe that limiting beliefs are real limits.

Your support team will surely remind you of your unlimited potential and possibilities.

Therefore, consider making agreements with your support team. For example, you might agree to meet one hour a week, or twenty minutes a week, depending on your schedules. During your meetings, you share what you are being *pulled to become*, and they share theirs. You discuss progress and obstacles. Other agreements could be a promise to not let each other down, to call regularly, to give and accept constructive criticisms, to be respectful at all times, and to redirect each other when one starts to engage in compromising activities that could undermine the attainment of one's *pull to become*. You meet with your support team knowing that you have one and only one intention—to be in the service of each member of the team and vice versa.

Your support team is 100 percent committed to your success. The team will act as your commitment device, meaning they will hold you accountable in a way that locks you into honoring your promise to yourself. Your team will help you avoid procrastination. They will uplift you and stand firmly with you when times are rough. So, ask yourself, what are your most pressing needs? In what areas do you experience the widest gap between your current condition and your *pull to become*? Know that the answer to closing this gap already exists. Others have done it, and so can you if you simply stay connected to your support team.

CHAPTER 7

ORGANIZED ASSETS

For every minute spent organizing, an hour is earned.

—Anonymous

Objectives

- Learners will be able to demonstrate understanding of personal assets and why it is important to organize them into useable forms, in a two-paragraph essay.
- Learners will be able to take inventory, list, and organize their assets into two categories: transferable and technical.
- Learners will be able to write two paragraphs to summarize the findings from Henry David Thoreau's "experiment with life," as well as its possible implication for achieving success.
- Learners will be able to apply what they have learned to help a friend prepare for a job interview.

Enduring Understandings

- You have unique skills and talents.
- It is important to explore, discover, and harness the power of these unique skills and talents.
- It is imperative to have a purpose to which you can apply these assets.

- You are sure to achieve beyond expectations when you direct your assets toward the attainment of your *pull to become.*
- Your success is a product of your desires, willingness, follow-up actions, associations, thought patterns, and assets.
- Thoreau's findings from his experiment provide a protocol for how to achieve success repeatedly.
- You are a co-creator with life.
- You are always creating—either by design or by default.
- Unwavering commitment is key to your success.

Essential Questions

- What are personal assets, and why is it important to organize them into useable forms for a specific goal?
- How will you organize your assets into useable forms that you can apply toward achieving a specific goal?
- What are the findings from Henry David Thoreau's "experiment with life?" Explain its possible implication for achieving success.
- How might you apply what you have learned in this chapter to help a friend organize his/her assets in preparation for a job interview?

College and Career Readiness Anchor Standards

- Reading Standards: R.CCR. 1, 2, 3, 4, 7, 8, 9, and 10.
- Writing Standards: W.CCR. 1, 2, 3, 4, 5, 6, 7, 8, 9, and 10.
- Speaking and Listening Standards:SL.CCR.1, 2, 3, 4, 5, and 6.
- Language Standards: L.CCR.1, 2, 3, 4, 5 and 6.

I N THIS CHAPTER, the focus is on an additional empowering tool to take with you on your expedition. We will organize your knowledge and skills into a coherent whole. This means you are going to consolidate your personal assets (skills, talents, interests, and experiences), your academic knowledge (acquired from formal schooling), as well as your new identity and self-concept. We are going to nickname your total assets as PAID (Personal, Academic, and Identity). Just as you carefully selected the members and created your support team, it is necessary for you to bring together all the assets that are relevant to your *pull to become,* no matter what it is for you. Thus, the objective of this chapter is to learn how to, and actually organize your PAID into a usable form, that you can then apply toward the achievement of your *pull to become.*

So, what do you know for sure about you and your PAID? In the discovery phase, you did some self-exploration and learned a lot about yourself. You wrote your findings down in your journal entry. Now it's time to go back and review the great work you have done. By now, you know your true identity. You understand that you are a divine being having a human experience. You are aware that you are far more than the physical body you can touch and feel. You know that you are more than your mistakes, stories, and whatever others have judged you to be. In fact, you now know that you are far more than you have ever thought yourself to be. The truth about you is that you are powerful, strong, smart, and capable of creating anything your mind can think of.

You are also aware that there is a *pull to become* tugging at your heart. This pull has been tugging at your heart for a long time. You feel it. Like the blade of grass that breaks through cement in search of sunshine, this *pull to become* wants to come out. It wants to break through and shine. It wants to become your reality—the life you are happy to live and experience on a daily basis. You know this because of your desire for a freer, fuller, and more expanded experience of life. You also know this because of your dissatisfaction with your current or past conditions. In my experience, this *pull to become* hounds until action is taken for it—it lets no one off the hook! You love the idea and the direction of the pull, but you don't know whether you can actually become what you are being pulled to become. Nevertheless, you have taken a leap of faith and decided to willingly advance toward what you feel *pulled to become* by undertaking this journey.

In the process, your *purpose for learning* has become clearer. In an earlier chapter, you learned that you are no accident but rather part of a grand design for life on this planet. You are aware that you are uniquely created for your purpose. You have a special contribution to this grand design called life. There is no one with your unique skills and talents—no one walking on the face of this earth who can make this contribution, but you. So, be reminded that there is nothing wrong with you, nothing missing in you. In fact, all your PAID are perfect and in order, just for the specific purpose you were created to fulfil right here on this earth.

By now, you have learned the power of productive and affirmative thinking. You have created a dependable support team, and now, you want to harness the power of your PAID assets into a comprehensive whole, so it's targeted, deliberate and focused. The intention here is to organize and use your PAID as an additional tool to empower you close the gap and achieve your *pull to become* in accelerated time. You know the power in you can overcome any thoughts of fear, lack, and limitation. You already know your support team is there for you whenever you hit a roadblock or when doubt and worry set in. You also understand that additional support is available to you from unexpected people and places. You realize that beneath your human condition is your larger, expanded, magnificent divine nature. This divine part of you is unlimited by any human conditions; it transcends time, space, and the confines of your physical body. It sees no limits in you, no matter how the facts and evidence stack up against you. Rather, it sees only opportunities and possibilities for you. It is forever for you and never against you! It will also support and empower you to achieve your *pull to become* if you want it bad enough.

So, consider this question: "How might you organize your assets into a coherent useable form?" Here are a few suggestions. First, take inventory of your assets – identity, personal characteristics, multiple intelligences, skills, interests and personality, core values, talents, academic strengths, experiences, etc. Second, summarize each of these in your journal entry. Third, categorize them into transferable and technical skills (revisit relevant sections of chapter 3 - tools to test whether your purpose for learning is right for you). Fourth, take a career inventory test to validate your *pull to become*. Fifth, conduct research to explore career and employment outlook, required qualifications, working conditions, etc. Lastly, use your creativity and genius mindset to formulate unique combinations of useable assets that you can then apply toward acquiring your dream job or realizing your *pull to become* in other domains of your life.

Throughout this chapter, we have used the word *apply* repeatedly. Having taken inventory and organized your PAID, how do you apply it toward the achievement of your pull to become? The *how* was revealed to the world in the year 1845 by an American philosopher, journalist, and poet, named Henry David Thoreau (HDT). At a very young age, HDT was very curious about life, and how it worked. He often wondered how it is that some people generated success repeatedly throughout their lives, and others died in the pursuit, never having achieved their highest potential. So, HDT conducted what he termed "an experiment with life." His intention was to understand life and how it worked, so much so that in his own words, he would "suck the marrow out of life"—meaning that he wanted to understand life so much that he could induce life to deliver to him whatever he wanted on his own terms. His experiment began when he decided to live "deliberately" away from civilization and socialization and in harmony with nature. At the age of twenty-eight, he built a cottage in the woods near Walden Pond in Concord, Massachusetts. History has it that he lived there "deliberately" for two years, two months, and two days. At the end of his experiment, he had this to say: *"I have learned this, at least, by my experiment.*

That if one advances confidently in the direction of his dreams and endeavors to live the life which he has imagined, he will meet with a success unexpected in common hours. He will put some things behind, will pass an invisible boundary; new, universal, and more liberal laws will begin to establish themselves around and within him; or the old laws be expanded, and interpreted in his favor in a more liberal sense, and he will live with the license of a higher order of beings."

Wow! When I first heard this, I was blown away, not only by its depth and profound nature but also by its wisdom, clarity, and precision. This is empowering!

So here it is. You now have in your toolbox what I would describe as the protocol for how to achieve your *pull to become* in accelerated time. Many successful people you may or may not know have used precisely this protocol or a variation of it to accomplish stupendous success in their undertakings. For ease of application, I will proceed to deconstruct this protocol as follows:

"If one ... This phrase signals a choice. Going for your *pull to become* is never mandatory—you do not have to yield to this pull. Know that you always have a choice. Life cannot do anything for you without your full cooperation. Success is self-initiated; you have to want it for you, your happiness and self-fulfillment. ... **advances** ... This means moving forward along the path of your pull to become— yielding to the pull and letting go of resistance. This also means you have to take deliberate action; you begin by taking the first step. Success requires a burning desire, as well as a willingness to do what is required ... **confidently** ... This means you do not allow the fear of the gap to cripple you. You do what you have to do, even in the face of fear. You gain confidence when you study, you trust the power of good, and you trust universal intelligence for guidance. You practice productive and affirmative thinking, you call on your support team, you harness your PAID, and you are confident that you have what it takes to succeed. Therefore, you keep stepping forward ... **in the direction of his dream** ... This means remaining persistent and focused on your *pull to become*, and *your purpose for learning*—not giving in to distractions or wavering ... **and endeavors to live the life which he has imagined** ... This means you try your best to live up to your pull to become - in the present moment, today, not at a future date. You don't have to be perfect at it, you just have to see yourself as it, act as if, step into this *pull to become* life, and live it now in whatever way you can ... **he will meet with a success unexpected in common hours** ... This means that success will most assuredly come your way, from surprising opportunities, people, places, and things, when you least expect them. You will find help, support and structure that you couldn't possibly have imagined was available to you, even in your everyday experience. **He will put some things behind** ... This means you will let go of some things, the old habits of being, doing, and thinking that no longer serve you. You will need to let go of some people, supposed friends, or even personal stories of victimhood. You will set aside frustration, anger, malice, resentment, and labels of any kind. You will forgive—yourself and any person who has ever harmed or said unkind things about you. You will give up worries, anxiety, superiority or inferiority complexes, thoughts of lack and limitations, etc. These are all dead weights, excess baggage that can slow you down on your journey toward your *pull to become*. **He will pass an invisible boundary** ... These boundaries represent the limits or borders we have placed on ourselves by our own thinking. They are phantom walls erected by fear thoughts and feelings of lack, limitations, or unworthiness. These boundaries are not real but imaginary. As we have learned, we can break through these seeming boundaries with productive and affirmative thinking, as well as a vivid imagination. Then countless opportunities show up **... as new, universal, and more liberal laws will begin to establish themselves around and within him** ... This means that all sorts of things will begin to work out in your favor. New rules, regulations, decrees, etc. that are supportive of you and the attainment of your *pull to become* will be put in place—you will get a "break," things will get easier, and the world will appear less complex and cold; more friendly and cooperative. You will recognize the seeds of opportunities in setbacks, and you will use them to your advantage ... **the old laws be expanded, and interpreted in his favor in a more liberal sense** ... Even the old, rigid laws will be made flexible and extended to accommodate your needs **... he will live with the license of a higher order of being** ... This means you will begin to live with authority and the freedom to go wherever you desire, and be, do, have or give whatever you want. You will move around with ease and dignity. You will wake up every day feeling good and grateful for the miracle of your very own life!

Henry David Thoreau closes with these words of encouragement: *"If you have built castles in the air, your work need not be lost; that is where they should be. Now put the foundations under them."* HDT is saying that if you have dreams for a bigger and brighter future, you have done the right thing. Keep up the vivid imagination. Next, go to work to transform your dreams into your reality. This is the call to action for all who desire to live the life of their *pull to become*. Anchor your *pull to become* right here on earth. It is doable—and now, you know how!

In reality, there is not a single person who will fail to achieve their *pull to become* after learning how to organize their PAID, and applying the wisdom of HDT's experiment to work in tandem with the law of good. This law of good is universal— meaning it is available to anyone who is open to receiving it and to the extent that they are willing to allow it. Imagine the law of good as the sun. It denies no one its warmth and light. However, you as an individual have to decide how much of the sun's benefits you want. You could open just one window in your house to allow in that much sunlight and warmth, or you could open all the doors and windows for more. Better yet, you could simply go outdoors, maybe go to the beach, and sunbathe! The choice is yours. For, as we reflect on our own experiences, the lives of the successful people we admire, and the way they achieved success; we will come to realize the timeless truth that success is possible for all, but achievable only by those who seek it with passion and persistence.

In conclusion, be reminded that you are the commander-in-chief (CIC) of your life. As the CIC, you may be wise to consider burning down any bridge to the past. According to history, Hernán Cortés, the Spanish commander during the Spanish–Mexico war, won that war in 1519 AD mainly because he burned down bridges. As soon as his men were inside Mexico, Cortes destroyed his ships, and he told his men, "There is no return—you will have to conquer or perish." So the soldiers knew they had to give it their all, defeat was not an option. Victory was the only choice—and guess what? They won! So march on, and don't look back. Continue to advance confidently, and you will meet with success, as HDT has assured. You have what it takes—productive thinking, a support team, a well-organized PAID, as well as the protocol for how it is done!

. . . . . .

CHAPTER 8

CLOSING THE GAP

Action plan—doubt, of whatever kind, can be ended by action alone.
—Bob Proctor

Objectives

- Learners will be able to write a five-paragraph essay to define an action plan, describe its elements and their importance, as well as construct arguments for creating an action plan.
- Learners will be able to create an action plan and explain how this action plan will help close the gaps between their current conditions and their *pull to become.*
- Learners will be able to write a paragraph to summarize what they have learned in this chapter.
- Learners will be able to apply what they have learned to help a friend bridge the gap separating them from their dreams.

Enduring Understandings

- Tugging at everyone's heart is a *pull to become* ....
- This pull will remain an intangible desire that will persist until you do something about it, i.e. take action for it.

- Creating an action plan helps you clearly see what you need to do, when and where you need to do it, and the resources you need to complete a task.
- An action plan also helps you monitor your progress along the way toward your *pull to become.*
- People do not plan to fail, they simply fail to plan.
- Placing your attention on your *pull to become* and away from self-doubts is one of the best ways to close the gap.

Essential Questions

- What is an action plan, its elements and their importance, as well as the advantages of having an action plan?
- How will you create an action plan? Explain how this action plan will help close the gap between your current condition and what you are being pulled to become.
- What did you learn from this chapter?
- How will you apply what you have learned to help a friend close the gap separating them from their dreams?

College and Career Readiness Anchor Standards

- Reading Standards: R.CCR. 1, 2, 3, 4, 7, 8, 9, and 10.
- Writing Standards: W.CCR. 1, 2, 3, 4, 5, 6, 7, 8, 9, and 10.
- Speaking and Listening Standards: SL.CCR.1, 2, 3, 4, 5, and 6.
- Language Standards: L.CCR.1, 2, 3, 4, 5 and 6.

I LOVE THE MESSAGE implicit in a cartoon I once read in a comic book. It depicted a man having a dream in which he saw a gigantic creature leaning over the foot of his bed as if about to grab him. Shaken and terrified, the man asked the monster, "What do you want to do with me?"

To this the creature replied, "I don't know. I am your dream— what do you want to do with me?"

That is the million-dollar question. What do you want to do with your dream—the *pull to become* that is tugging at your heart? What are you going to do with the pull toward a healthier life style? What are you going to do with the possibility of the bigger, brighter, and more fulfilling life that awaits you and which you now see on your horizon? The cartoon referenced above suggests that some of us see images of dark, grotesque, ugly creatures haunting us, even in our dreams. Thankfully, that is not the case for you. Your *pull to become* bears an altruistic, happy, and fulfilling perspective of life. It is big, and it is perfect just for you. However, what are you going to do with this generous and beneficial *pull to become*? Remember, you cannot run away from your *pull to become*. As the cartoon suggests, it will continue to hound you, even in your sleep, until you do something with it. What will you do with your *pull to become*— resist it or lean into it?

My guess is that you want to lean-in, embrace, and act on it. You want to achieve this *pull to become*—you want to experience it as the life you love living now. So, you will take deliberate actions in support of your *pull to become*. Therefore, the focus of this chapter is to emphasize the importance of an action plan, learning how to create an effective action plan, and shedding light on the importance of following through with the specific tasks in an action plan that will enable closing the gap.

Your action plan is simply a document written by you that describes the way you will achieve your pull to become through detailed action steps. Creating a detailed action plan is in your best interest; it can help turn your *pull to become* into your reality by keeping you focused and accountable. Your action plan is comparable to a bridge that could connect you to your desires. If you walk diligently along this bridge, you are sure to arrive at your destination. You can monitor your progress as you undertake each task step-by-step. In addition, action plans can increase your efficiency by helping you save time, energy, and resources. For example, you can prioritize the amount of time you spend on each task, thereby preventing distractions that might occur. In some way, your action plan represents a commitment to yourself that indicates you are serious about transforming your *pull to become* into reality by closing the gap.

Remember that wise saying: "People don't plan to fail. Rather, they fail to plan." Having come this far, I bet you certainly do not want to fail. You want to live the new life that is tugging at your heart. You want to make it your reality – the life you love living. You want to succeed. You want to be happy, peaceful, and fulfilled. Therefore, the time is now! It makes sense to begin right now to develop your action plan. This action plan is your blueprint for the journey toward your *pull to become*. It represents how you plan to navigate the gap. It does not have to be perfect right now. Your action plan is always a work in progress. As you embark on this journey, your vision – your *pull to become*, is likely to evolve and expand and so will your *purpose for learning*. So, keep your plan handy and visible, as a constant reminder and guide. Keep an open mind!

An effective action plan consists of several action steps that answer the following questions:

- What action steps (tasks) must I take?
- When will I begin taking these action steps (time line)?
- What resources (money, time, transportation, etc.) do I need?
- Who should know about my plan (communication)?

When you create your action plan, make sure it is complete, clear, and current. Try not to overlook any detail. Remember to list all the necessary action steps. This will immediately reveal what you may be able to do on your own and where you will need help, as well as the type of help you will need. Leave room for emergencies. It is also important that you prioritize the tasks and set a definite date by which you intend to accomplish the tasks. Consider for example, that it is springtime, and you want to go part time on your current job so you can return to school in the fall semester and complete your college education. Your action plan might look like this:

	WHAT (Tasks)	WHEN (Timeline)	RESOURCES	COMMUNICATION (How)
1	Reapply for fall admission.	March 1, 2018	-College admission website	Support team/ social and professional networks
2	Share admission letter and intent to go part time with supervisor.	June 1, 2018	-Admission letter	Support team/ social and professional networks
3	Seek part-time job opportunities with current employer.	June 1, 2018	-All appropriate announcements for job openings -Trusted supervisors/ employees, colleagues, etc.	Support team/ social and professional networks
4	Seek part-time job opportunities with other employers.	June 1, 2018	-Internet search - Newspaper job announcements - Support team etc.	Support team/ social and professional networks
5	Prepare for interview - update resume - do mock interviews - gather information about company, its location, travel time, etc. -clothing	As soon as invited	- Videos on interviewing skills - Web-based help with resume writing - Support team - Company website - Business review sites - Money	Support team/ social and professional networks
6	Start part-time job	August 1, 2018	-Skills, talents, positive mental attitude	Support team/ social and professional networks
7	Start school	September 2018	-Books, electronic devices, etc., diligence, hard work	Support team/ social and professional networks

8	Take final exams	May 2019	-Books, electronic devices, etc., diligence, hard work	Support team/ social and professional networks
9	Celebrate graduation	June 2019	-Money, camera, party venue, etc.	Support team, family, friends, and other well-wishers

Now, take some time to create an action plan that will enable you to close the gap between your current condition and what you are being pulled to become (revisit some of the gaps you identified in chapter 4). Next, take your plan and go to work! This is called follow-through. It means you begin to do what you say that you are going to do, as stated in your action plan.

Follow-through is what two teenage boys did when they planned to outsmart the village wise man so they could gain the respect and admiration of everyone in the village. The whole community admired and honored this man because he is knowledgeable and full of wisdom. So, thinking they were smarter than the wise man, the two boys crafted a detailed action plan to fool him in the presence of the entire community. They planned to secure an appointment with the wise man, publicize the appointment, capture a live bird, and show up at the appointment with the live bird. During the meeting with the wise man, they planned that one boy will hold the live bird in his hands, behind his back, and the other boy will stand very close to the one holding the bird to block the view of the wise man and prevent him from seeing the bird. Then, the teenager holding the bird will ask the wise man whether the bird he is holding is alive or dead. If the wise man says the bird is alive, he will quickly squeeze the life out of it and present the dead bird, thereby proving him wrong. If, however, the wise man says the bird is dead, then he shall just present the bird, and they will have outsmarted the wise man, and the villagers will look up to them instead of the wise man.

Having created their plan, they proceeded to act on it— they followed through, or carried out their plans. They made the appointment. They informed the whole community, so the whole community showed up for this meeting. The boys captured a live bird and took it with them to the appointment. Standing in front of the wise man, the teenage boys politely asked him if the bird one of them is holding is alive or dead.

As the story goes, the wise man looked very compassionately at the two young boys, and with a knowing smile said to them, "The life you are holding in your hands is yours." What a wise and profound response! Reflect on it for a moment and see what you make of it. What does it mean for you to recognize that the life you are holding in your hands, that the life you are living is completely up to you? This means you can mold and shape it into any form you want based on the actions you take. Because the teenage boys followed through on their action plans, they received much more than they had bargained for. They learned a valuable life lesson— that their life is in their hands. They could crush it or nurture it by their own actions. So it is with you and me! We could crush or actualize our *pull to become* more by our very own actions. The life that each one of us is living depends on our choices, action plans, and follow-through. So, to what extent are you willing to undertake and complete the tasks in your action plan? How much do you want what you want? Remember this: experts suggest that success is 20 percent planning for success and 80 percent following through or acting on your plans. What actions are you going to take today in support of your *pull to become*? Know that when you take action, life will always give you much more than you had hoped for. The teenage boys wanted respect; life gave them much more – wisdom!

So, by now, you have crafted a detailed action plan and shared it with your support team for their input. Again, if you have not yet developed an action plan, please STOP right here and do so! Solicit suggestions from your support team and let them know how you integrated their feedbacks. They will feel good about this and will be more likely to contribute in the future. Now you are ready to take the calculated risk and leap into the gap, navigate it with the intention to close it. As you take deliberate action steps toward your *pull to become*, remember to apply HDT's protocol. In addition, monitor your progress. Keep track of what you have done and what remains to be done. Celebrate your accomplishments along the way.

Although you are aware of your constant companion – fear, you have learned how to handle fear. You acknowledge it, evaluate its credibility, do what is required, and then, you go on with your plan. You understand that you need to tame your fear by removing your attention from it, so that eventually, it will shrink and rendered powerless over you. You also understand that you need to expand your capacity by placing your attention on completing the tasks in your action plan. Along the way, you remind yourself that wherever you place your attention, there flows your energy. So, you place your attention on your optimistic future and not the detractor – fear, because your attention informs life about what it is that you want. This is very important to note. If you focus your attention on what you don't want, life delivers it anyway. Why? Because of the law of *cause and effect* that has no mind of its own. This law only knows to deliver your desire, and it recognizes your desire by where you place your attention. The law of cause and effect responds to the patterns of thoughts that you hold in your mind. This causes you to experience whatever dominates your thinking. This is an immutable law, much like the law of the farm: what you sow is what you reap. If you plant, and nurture orange seeds, you reap oranges. Likewise, if you place your attention on fear, you will reap fear-filled results - confusion, worry, anxiety, etc.

You understand that fear is an unavoidable part of this journey, but be aware that as you undertake and complete task after task on your action plan, fear becomes less of a deterrent. Remember that you are very powerful—much more than you know! You are so powerful that with your belief, you can say to life, *"I want this pull to become,"* and because you are taking actions that support your belief, life will conspire with all the forces of nature to deliver this *pull to become* to you, as ordered or even better. On the other hand, if you give in to fear, procrastination, doubt, or all the things that could go wrong, all the things that could go wrong will go wrong. So, follow through on your action plans and trust life. Your *pull to become* will definitely become your reality. And if you really want to achieve your *pull to become* in accelerated time, then you will turn your attention away from fear and place it on belief—not once or twice but repeatedly, all the time! When you do so, you will see dynamic and dramatic results, even with some mistakes along the way. You don't have to be perfect. Just begin, even with your imperfections, and know you will succeed, because life will support you.

Fear thoughts are often persistent! Along the way to your *pull to become*, fear thoughts will show up uninvited, tag along, and demand to engage you in unproductive and endless mind chatter. If you refuse to give in to this demand, eventually the fear thoughts will recede to the background and no longer able to dominate your thinking or control your choices. Therefore, when fear thoughts, such as the *What ifs* ... arise; just tell yourself you will handle it. Remind yourself that you have support – life will support you. That your desire to succeed and the willingness to do what it takes will elevate and strengthen you. It is at these *What if* moments that that you make a conscious decision to redirect your thoughts away from what could go wrong and place your thoughts on what you can do today in support of your *pull to become*. I encourage you to hold your action plan firmly in your mind. Know that it is not in the absence of fear that you will succeed and achieve your dreams. In fact, never in recorded history has fear been known to step aside voluntarily for dream seekers to navigate the gap successfully. Rather, it is taking action in the presence of some fear. Achieving your *pull to become* is not about being perfect or about knowing how everything is going to work out. It is about facing your fear, taking the initial baby steps into the gap, and then advancing confidently toward your *pull to become* as Thoreau suggested. When we do this repeatedly even in the face of fear and disappointments, success is inevitable.

PART III

TRANSFORMATION

Nothing happens until the pain of remaining the
same outweighs the pain of change.

—Arthur Burt

Thus far, you have done a lot of work. Welcome back, and good job for staying the course! You are now stepping into the transformation phase - the last phase of our journey together. To get to this phase, you went through the discovery phase—in which you did all the early work of exploring and discovering your true *identity, pull to become, purpose for learning,* and the fear-filled *gap.* Then you stepped into the empowerment phase, wherein you learned tools that enable you to navigate and close the gap between your current condition and what you are being pulled to become. This brings you to the transformation phase—the stage at which you acknowledge the changes that are taking place in you as a result of undertaking this journey.

This journey has been a long one. Days, weeks, and even months may have gone by since you began. This is by no means a walk in the park. Although it has been very challenging at times, you understand that your *pull to become* is well worth it. The transformative benefit of undertaking this journey is amazing; it can be likened to the life cycle of a butterfly that begins with an egg on a leaf. After a while, the egg hatches into a caterpillar. The caterpillar is active, constantly eating leaves and flowers. Because it eats so much, it grows rapidly and loses its old skin many times to accommodate this growth. Once its insatiable appetite has been quelled, the caterpillar travels long distances to find a place to rest (the chrysalis stage). There it transforms into a beautiful creature no longer shackled to the earth. Now, it can fly, it is free. We recognize this new creature as the colorful butterfly. By taking this course, you too have engaged with an incredible opportunity to transform your life. You have learned to break free from the shackles of the past that up until now kept you contained, constricted, and powerless. Like the butterfly, you have emerged into a magnificent new you. Figuratively, you have developed wings and acquired the empowering knowledge that you too can soar to unimaginable heights.

CHAPTER 9

RESILIENCE

Success is not final; failure is not fatal: it is the courage to continue that counts.
—Winston Churchill

Objectives

- Learners will be able to share an experience of personal resilience orally, or in written form.
- Learners will be able to do a book, movie, or media review evaluating how different characters demonstrated resilience in the face of hardship.
- Learners will be able to summarize what they have learned in this chapter about resilience.
- Learners will be able to apply what they have learned to solve real-life challenges related to achieving their *pull to become.*

Enduring Understandings

- Resilience—the ability to come back after a setback—is a characteristic common to all successful people.
- "Tough times never last, but tough people do." (Robert Schuller)
- No one is immune to disappointments. Life has a way of throwing all kinds of dirt—shame, betrayal, misfortune, ill health, loss of reputation, loss of freedom, loss of job, etc.,—on all.

- How you choose to respond when all hope seems lost will define you. It will determine whether you are a winner or a quitter.
- Consider every "failure" as a fountain of information.
- It is important to realize that there is, and there has to be a solution to any problem or obstacle!

Essential Questions

- What is resilience?
- How have you demonstrated resilience in your experiences?
- What have you learned about resilience in this chapter?
- How might you apply what you have learned to solve challenges along the way to your *pull to become?*

College and Career Readiness Anchor Standards

- Reading Standards: R.CCR. 1, 2, 3, 4, 7, 8, 9, and 10.
- Writing Standards: W.CCR. 1, 2, 3, 4, 5, 6, 7, 8, 9, and 10.
- Speaking and Listening Standards: SL.CCR.1, 2, 3, 4, 5, and 6.
- Language Standards: L.CCR.1, 2, 3, 4, 5 and 6.

R ESILIENCE IS ONE of the many transformational benefits of this journey. Resilience simply means the ability to come back after a setback—being able to recover from adversity, failure, or being beaten down by life. In essence, it's when you've morphed into the "comeback kid." Resilience is a characteristic common to all successful people. If you take the time to read their biographies, you will discover that they all had their fair share of failures. Rather than quit, they worked through these tough times and succeeded. They realized that in order to succeed they had to outlast the tough times. It was the late Robert Schuller who once said, "Tough times never last, but tough people do." So, toughness or resilience is one or the many attributes you gain by undertaking this journey. As you already know, challenges will arise, obstacles will show up, and you might even fall multiple times on your journey toward your *pull to become*. Nevertheless, you will rise up again and again and go after what you want. Doing so is what makes you resilient.

I learned to appreciate resilience first-hand from observing a toddler many years ago. This toddler was my eleven-month-old son learning to walk and to get to the things he desired more quickly. I recall him crawling on his hands and knees but wanting to walk on his feet, just like other family members around him. Soon he learned to pull himself up by holding onto a square ottoman we had in the living room. As long as he was holding on to the ottoman, he could actually walk around it. One day, I deliberately sat across the room from him and held up a bright red-and-yellow toy car. I dangled the toy car and gestured that he come get it. As soon as his eyes caught the toy, I could see he was excited and pulled by a desire to get to the toy. I could also sense his dissatisfaction: he was stuck at the ottoman, and he wanted this toy as soon as possible. Seeing that other family members were moving around quickly on two feet, he wanted to do just the same. So, he decided to let go of the ottoman, took a couple of steps and he fell down. He crawled back to the ottoman, pulled himself back up, and again took two more steps before he fell down a second time. This scenario played out repeatedly, and we practiced this routine on a daily basis until he eventually mastered his balance and walked over to the toy car.

Observing his efforts was very insightful to me, and since then, I have become more aware that taking new steps and going for what you want is not difficult only for a toddler but for all ages. Moreover, although my son fell down repeatedly, never once did I see him give up. Instead, what I observed was resilience – he got up repeatedly until he achieved his desire to walk and reach what he wanted– in this case a bright red and yellow toy car.

Imagine that you've received an F grade in math, and you say, "That's it! I guess I'm not just good in math." You carry this notion with you for life, avoiding any opportunity to reverse this misguided belief. Or maybe you do poorly in a semester, get fired from a job, break up with a boyfriend or girlfriend, or fall down in some regard, and then you give up on your *pull to become*. This need not be so. You have to want your *pull to become* so badly that no obstacle or disappointment can deter you. You have to be resilient, to try, try, and try again. Get help if you need it, but do not quit. The question is, do you have grit, or are you a quitter? I have heard it said that quitters don't win, and winners don't quit! If you want to win, you must develop resilience—the ability to rise up over and over again from a knock down, a "failure," and continue toward your *pull to become* and never looking back.

As you think about resilience, consider the lesson in this popular fable. One day, a farmer's donkey fell down into a well. The animal cried out in distress for hours as the farmer tried to figure out what to do. Eventually, the farmer decided the animal was old, and the well needed to be covered up anyway, so it just wasn't worth it to rescue the donkey. He asked some neighbors to come over and help him. They each grabbed a shovel and began to shovel dirt into the well. Realizing what was occurring, the donkey cried out in anguish, but soon calmed down to everyone's consternation.

Upon looking down the well to gauge the progress being made, the farmer was astounded to discover that the donkey is shaking off the dirt and using it as leverage to step up. Surely enough, the donkey stepped out of the well and went about his merry way. Isn't that an inspiring story? The truth is that at some point, life is going to shovel dirt and throw many curves at you, me, and anyone else. There are all kinds of dirt and curves: shame, betrayal, misfortune, ill-health, loss of reputation, loss of freedom, loss of job, etc. You will come across disappointments along the path of your *pull to become*. Like the donkey, the trick is to shake off the disappointment and use the experience to step up in the direction of what you want to *be* and *do*. Consider every failure as a stepping stone, a springboard of information from which to launch yourself forward. We can get out of the deepest wells in our lives by simply refusing to give up—by staying resilient!

Suppose you are doing everything you have learned in this course. You invest your time and energy, you study, you follow your action plan, you work closely with your support team, etc. You face and overcome obstacles, and yet as time goes on, your *pull to become* is just not showing up the way you want it to, and in a timely manner. It feels as though the more you do, the more there is to do – a never-ending pursuit. Consequently, you are feeling exhausted, frustrated and really, really tempted to just give up, because you absolutely do not know what more you can possibly do. Then what? Do you abandon the pursuit and accept failure? My answer is no! As hard as it may be to accept, you must understand that sometimes, regardless of hard work and due diligence, things may not work out as planned. At such times, be reminded that what we may perceive as failure is most often something else. It may be premium information, an important feedback, much like your mid-semester grade. It is not your final grade, and there is usually some opportunities hidden in the experience of perceived failure. You may be receiving valuable information to find new study partners or support team; quit procrastinating, ditching classes, etc. You may be receiving a signal to get clear about what you think you are being *pulled to become*. Perhaps, the seeming failure is quality information for the purpose of redirecting you to something much bigger and better for you.

So, in moments of frustration and uncertainties, know that you have choices. One is to give up, and the other is to be resilient, to try, try, and try again. If you do so, you open up a space for more ideas, opportunities, and support from unexpected people and places. I encourage you to stay in the pursuit; an opportunity will definitely show up. Challenges are inevitable—everyone faces challenges, and life pours dirt on all! However, you will be defined by how you choose to respond when things appear rough and tough. This will determine whether you are a resilient individual or a quitter.

Understand that there is no problem without a solution, no question without an answer—whether this be in math, physics, civics, work, relationships, or life itself. So it is with the law of creating: there is nothing you can think of that you cannot create, nothing that you can see that you cannot be. There has to be a pathway to achieving what you are pulled to become. This is affirmative thinking in action, and practicing it helps you become more resilient, refusing to let problems dominate you and your thinking. Otherwise, it's tempting to always focus on the obstacle. It is imperative to turn inward to "re-mind" yourself that there is an answer! Remain in this productive and affirmative thinking space, and an answer will surely show up at the right time and place. Even if you choose to give up on that *pull to become*, your choice will be made from a place of wisdom and guidance, and not from a place of fear.

It's human to get tired at times, to think, this is just too much work, too hard, and I don't want to do this anymore. Or you may hit those moments when you don't know whether to abandon or to endure. Whenever I reach this confusing point on my own journey, I remind myself of the advice from my friend Mary Morrissey who taught me to speak these words to myself: *"Boundless wisdom, if this pull to become is for my higher good, increase my passion for it. I am open to an idea. Give me an idea to move me forward. However, if this pull to become will not benefit others and me, decrease my energy for it, and redirect me. I am open to this or something better."* These words have helped to keep me relaxed even in the face of disappointment and frustration. I invite you to try it for yourself and see what happens. Otherwise, you can take a temporary break from the work while at the same time, asking for guidance from life. *"What new information might make a difference? Who could I talk to?"* Asking these questions might help you to generate different ideas to solve the problem.

To help you stay in the game at moments of frustration and disappointment, consider how the following famous people used the quality of resilience to overcome challenges.

Michael Jordan (MJ). Many consider MJ to be the greatest basketball player in the world. However, it is instructive to know that he was cut from his high school varsity basketball team. This experience had devastated him. For some, this would have meant the death of their dream - their *pull to become*. This was not the case for MJ. Public records suggest that the experience strengthened his resolve to work harder and strive higher. This led to the attainment of the high level of success for which he is famous. Speaking to the concept of resilience, MJ indicated that he missed more than nine thousand shots in his career, and that he must have lost nearly three hundred games. Further, he was entrusted to take the game-winning shot which he missed on more than twenty-six different occasions. Rather than bowing his head and giving up, this only motivated him to work harder. Indeed, this is resilience!

Steve Jobs was reportedly fired from Apple, the company he founded. He also failed with NeXT Computer Company and the Lisa computer. Later, he went back to Apple, and led the business to become one of the most profitable companies in the United States.

Walt Disney was purportedly the artist that no one wanted to hire. It is believed he was unable to get a job elsewhere and his brother was only able to secure a temporary job for him. His first animation studio went bankrupt. However, he persevered, and co-founded *The Walt Disney*. It is reported that the company had over $40 billion in revenue in 2012.

Records in public domain has it that **Steven Spielberg** twice applied to attend the film school at the University of Southern California (USC). His application was denied both times. He remained undeterred in the pursuit of his dreams. Spielberg has grossed $8.5 billion from Films that he has directed. In recognition of his success, USC awarded him an honorary degree. Further, he later became a trustee of the University.

Charles Schultz's drawings were reportedly rejected by his high school yearbook staff. Schultz eventually created Peanuts (featuring Snoopy and Charlie Brown). The cartoon and licensing/product revenue from Peanuts generated over $1 billion a year for nearly fifty years. Not surprising, his high school that had previously rejected his drawings put a statue of Snoopy in the main office.

It's been widely reported that **Colonel Harland Sanders** was a sixth-grade dropout. At the age of sixty-five, a new interstate highway diverted traffic away from his restaurant. This left Sanders with only his secret fried chicken recipe and a social security check. He resorted to selling his recipe and franchise idea. According to public records, he was rejected over one thousand times. Later, he found a partner with whom he built the KFC franchise powerhouse. KFC now has over fifteen thousand restaurants in the United States.

Mary Kay Ash reportedly sold books from one home to the other while her husband was in the military. Unfortunately, they divorced leaving her with three children at a time when divorce was frowned upon. It is reported that she was passed over for a promotion because she was a woman. She later remarried and with her second husband planned a business, Mary Kay Cosmetics. She suffered another loss when her husband died one month prior to the launching of this business venture. Her eldest son came to the rescue with a five-thousand-dollar investment. Ash was able to use this to launch her business. Forbes reported 2014 revenue as over $3.5 billion.

Public records alleged that **Oprah Winfrey** was fired from her job co-anchoring the 6:00PM News at Baltimore's WJZ because she was not the right fit. In her own public discussions about occurrences at another job, she indicated that she was warned she could be fired because she involved herself in other people's stories rather than simply reporting the stories. Oprah refused to change her compassionate nature for the sake of a job. She was resilient, followed her heart, and went on to host the highest-ranked TV show of its kind. Oprah now owns her television network called *OWN*. She became a billionaire, and she is also a remarkable philanthropist that gets involved in other people's stories to help them live their best life.

Public records indicate that **Jack Canfield** was rejected 144 times before he found a publisher for his book, *Chicken Soup for the Soul*. His publisher thought he was out of touch with reality when he suggested that he aspired to sell 1.5 million books in the first eighteen months. It is on record that his first book sold more than eight million copies in America and ten million copies worldwide. Canfield's advice is that people should be more committed to their vision than other people's doubt or fear.

J.K. Rowlings spoke about failures during a graduation ceremony at Harvard University. In her address to new graduates, she drew attention to the numerous failures that she had experienced in her life. More importantly, she indicated that "it is impossible to live without failing at something, unless you live so cautiously that you might as well not have lived at all - in which case, you failed by default." It is reported that several publishers rejected the manuscript of her book, *Harry Porter*, before one finally agreed to publish it.

However, the publisher advised Rowlings that she needed to get a job, since there was no money in children's books. She is now a billionaire from the success of Harry Porter.

Mark Cuban, the billionaire entrepreneur, brilliantly captured the essence of resilience in these words: "it doesn't matter how many times you fail, you only have to be right once." He indicated that he tried to sell powdered milk and was literally an idiot a lot of times. However, he never gave up. He learned from all his failures, making him the successful entrepreneur that he is today.

We can go on and on about famous failures and examples of resilience. I believe you can find many more examples of your own— from your experiences and those of your parents, grandparents, neighbors, friends, etc. Reflect on these, and find resilience everywhere around you. You are part of it, in it, and have it in you! Activating this power of resilience in you is one of the most significant benefits you gain from taking this course. It's not that you seek failure, but along the way to the realization of your *pull to become*, things will happen that you can't predict, plan, or prepare for. The way you handle these unforeseen circumstances, obstacles, or setbacks will determine whether you succeed or fail, win or lose.

The people who win in the end are the ones who tough it out. The late Robert Schuller characterized the winners "as the folks who remain focused, forge ahead by either burrowing through the obstacle, rising above it, stooping to conquer it, or sidestepping it altogether." Regardless of how many times they are knocked down, they rise up, dust off, and carry on. They tough it out. They are determined to win, and they win! Each setback only strengthens their resolve—it makes them stronger, more determined, and resilient.

What is it that enables people to show incredible courage and resilience in the face of adversity? This question was answered by Dr. Dennis Charney and his associates at Yale University. After many years of working with military veterans who suffered post-traumatic stress disorder (PTSD) and depression, they decided to shift their research focus to people who had been traumatized but who had not developed PTSD, depression, or substance-abuse problems. Their findings culminated in what he termed "a prescription for resilience." According to the work of Dr. Charney and associates, resilient people

- tap into their prior experience to help them get through the current challenges;
- are prepared to work outside their comfort zone as needed;
- seek support from others when they need help and do not wait for help to arrive;
- are courageous and able to overcome fear by acting despite being afraid;
- are optimistic, tending to have a positive outlook on life and laughing a lot, not just at themselves but at everyday occurrences, by reframing situations and experiences;
- have a strong set of core moral values, help others, rely on faith, and believe in a higher power;
- have role models and support teams that offer strength and encouragement during tough times; and
- live lives of meaning, of purpose, with a mission—they live deliberately!

Dr. Charney concluded that one can become resilient through training or through experience in meeting and overcoming challenges. So, although resilient people typically exhibit the characteristics listed above— usually positive and upbeat, able to go it alone and never give up—the reality is that resilient people experience most of the problems that non-resilient people experience. The major difference between a resilient and a non-resilient person is how quickly resilient people recover from failures and setbacks in their lives. Resilient people speedily bounce back from adversity. Resilient and truly happy people understand the meaning of good enough. They know when to stop and enjoy what they have achieved without dwelling on disappointments. They live in the present and enjoy life as it is, even as they work toward their *pull to become* and do more with their lives.

This chapter closes with these wishes for you: May you have enough happiness to make you sweet, enough hope to make you dream, and enough trials to make you resilient. Be reminded that the most successful people you know have had their fair share of knockdowns as well. Rather than give up, they get up, dust-off, and step up. They are resilient. And so are you!

CHAPTER 10

OPEN-MINDEDNESS

A mind is like a parachute. It doesn't work if it is not open.

—Frank Zappa

Objectives

- Learners will be able to demonstrate understanding of the concept of open-mindedness through oral communication, visual arts, cartoons, prose, drama, essay, etc.
- Learners will be able to cite evidence of open- or closed-mindedness of a character in a given piece of literature.
- Learners will be able to write a paragraph summarizing what they have learned about open-mindedness in this chapter.
- Learners will be able to write a two-paragraph essay explaining how they might apply the content learned to enhance their ability to achieve their *pull to become.*

Enduring Understandings

- Open-mindedness requires that we remain receptive to new ideas, information, concepts, etc., without attachments.
- The "I-know-it-all" attitude is dangerous in that it could lead to arrogance.

- One of the many benefits of open-mindedness is the realization that to achieve a *pull to become*, one must start with a beginner's mind—a mind that is curious, open to everything, and closed to nothing.
- More good will be noticeable everywhere when the mind is open to all possibilities.

Essential Questions

- What is open-mindedness, and what does it mean for an individual to be open-minded?
- How can you assert that a character is open-or closed-minded in a given piece of literature?
- What did you learn about open-mindedness in this chapter?
- How might you apply what you have learned to enhance your curiosity and flexibility?

College and Career Readiness Anchor Standards

- Reading Standards: R.CCR. 1, 2, 3, 4, 7, 8, 9, and 10.
- Writing Standards: W.CCR. 1, 2, 3, 4, 5, 6, 7, 8, 9, and 10.
- Speaking and Listening Standards: SL.CCR.1, 2, 3, 4, 5, and 6.
- Language Standards: L.CCR.1, 2, 3, 4, 5 and 6.

T HERE IS A story about a famous scientist who went to a Sage in search of the secret of life. This scientist was renowned for his breakthrough discoveries in the biological sciences and medicine. He had received many accolades and prestigious honors for his innovations and contributions to the advancement of science. He also held the patents for over a thousand inventions. He had invested his money wisely too. Consequently, this man was not only wealthy and well educated; he was also well respected worldwide. He had travelled the world and visited many notable destinations. Socially, he was highly connected and was friends with many of the powerful people of the world. This man was successful and famous by all accounts, and in his mind, he had accomplished everything except for one thing: knowledge of the secret of life. So he began his search for the secret of life. This was how he heard about the Hindu sage who knew the secret. He decided to meet with this sage, so he set up an appointment.

On the day of his appointment, he arrived early. Not long afterward, he was ushered in to meet with the sage. The sage offered him tea and the scientist accepted the offer. Then, the famous scientist asked for an assurance that the sage will tell him the secret of life after pouring the tea. The sage agreed. The sage then brought out the teapot and two teacups, one for the scientist and the other for himself. He took the teapot and began to pour out the tea, while looking at this man, who was narrating his accomplishments. The sage kept pouring the tea. It filled the teacups, and the tea overflowed into the saucers and table cloth, down the sides of the table, and onto the man's suit and feet. Suddenly, the scientist felt the hot tea on his legs. He quickly stood up and informed the sage that the cups are full and can hold no more.

The sage looked at him, and he said, *"So is your mind … it is full and can hold no more. A cup can only be filled when it is empty, and you too, can only be filled when you are empty. Come back when your mind is empty, when you are not so full of yourself, and you will know the secret of life."*

How interesting? What can we learn from this story? Yes, that it is important to be open-minded—meaning a willingness to be open and receptive to new ideas. This way, we are able to learn and grow in wisdom and understanding. If we are filled with the attitude of "I know it all," it will be difficult to grow and learn the things that we need in order to be successful and achieve our *pull to become.* The *I-know-it-all* attitude will blind us from seeing what we need in order to learn and understand. Open-mindedness simply requires a mind that is open to everything and attached to nothing. Some people call it the beginner's mindset; it is empty, free of habits of "I know it all" or "I have been there, done that," and ready to accept, doubt, and be equally open to all possibilities. The man in the story was so full of himself and his achievements that he had no room for more learning. He had no room even for the thing he desired the most. He was unwilling, at least temporarily, to set aside all of his accomplishments, be quiet, and listen to the sage for the very secret he yearned to discover.

On this adventure leading toward your *pull to become,* you have learned the value of open-mindedness, to have a bigger space in you to accommodate the good, the bad, as well as the unpleasant experiences along the way to achieving your *pull to become.* You are becoming more flexible and adaptable - willing to grow and revise your thinking, action plan, purpose for learning, etc. as necessary. You know better than to think you already know everything you need to know. You are open-minded enough to know that there are valuable lessons to be learned in every chapter of this book, and that collectively; they provide the insight, guidance and support necessary to accomplish your *pull to become* in accelerated time. Open-mindedness has brought you this far, remain open to more possibilities for your life.

So, remember to develop no attachment to any person, place, or thing on this journey. Instead, be open and completely willing to be redirected to a *pull to become* a bigger and better version of yourself. Be reminded that it is the nature of life to forever seek to grow and expand in, through and as you. It is the will of life for you to play big, achieve big, and give big. It is the will of life for you to be free, successful, peaceful and happy. It is the will of life for you to be healthy, feel whole and complete. Therefore, learn to open up to the idea of *"this, or something more!"* For, it is only through your willingness to open up your mind to receiving success and happiness that success and happiness will become your reality. Allow things to freely flow in and through your life without attempting to hold on too strong. No matter what the situation may be, let things come and go as they may without attachments. Then, trust that the law of good will always act on the idea of "this, or something more" and deliver to you this or something more always.

You have made a decision for your *pull to become*. This is something that matters to you, and that means you are committed to keeping an open mind. And, in the event that you are redirected, it will always be for something bigger and better, because life has only one thing in store for you, and that is your highest good. Remember, we don't want to get so attached to a *pull to become* that we eliminate other possibilities, other ideas that actually may be bigger and better for us. Instead, we simply speak it, and then release it, and trust that it will return to us fulfilled because it will be acted upon by the law of good that only knows to deliver good.

So, the transformation here is open-mindedness! The mind that welcomes all possibilities. You've learned that to realize your *pull to become* you must start with a beginner's mind, a mind that is curious, open to everything, and closed to nothing. This is the attitude of humility and a willingness to change because you undertook this journey. Open-mindedness has enabled you to trust the process. On this adventure it may look at first as if nothing is happening and that you are not making progress. You are working hard, putting in a lot of time and effort, but there are no visible results. Even so, keep your mind open to the possibility that this may be the incubation period— just like the chrysalis phase in the life cycle of the butterfly - that period when you notice only a very little or no progress externally.

Nevertheless, tremendous changes are taking place internally. You are becoming more open-minded. Open-mindedness will enable you to honor this period, no matter how short or long. Over time, you will see the results. So honor every step you have taken toward your *pull to become*. Look for any signs of progress, recognize and celebrate them. Yes, savor what is happening along the way— the by-products of your pull to become. This means tasting and enjoying the experience of this journey. Really, notice the good things that are in your life right now and those that have occurred along the way. Maybe a new attitude – embrace it. Maybe a new friend or study partner—give thanks. Perhaps a fresh perspective occurred to you— be curious about it. As you move closer and closer to your *pull to become*, notice that you will find more and more experiences to celebrate. You will notice more good in your life when your mind remains open to all possibilities.

CHAPTER 11

CONFIDENCE

*Don't be satisfied with stories, how things have gone
with others. Unfold your own myth.*

—Rumi

Objectives

- Learners will be able to demonstrate understanding of the concept of confidence through various forms of self-expression: read aloud, public speaking, active listening, recollecting, writing, reasoning, etc.
- Learners will be able to write a four-paragraph descriptive essay about the different levels of confidence, giving specific examples for each level.
- Learners will be able to summarize what they have learned about confidence.
- Learners will be able to apply what they learned to increase their confidence in their ability to achieve their *pull to become.*

Enduring Understandings

- Confidence means following your *pull to become* and not the crowd.
- You are no longer held back by history, fear, doubt and stories of victimhood.

- You realize that there is no question without an answer, no problem without a solution, and that life is on your side, etc.
- Confidence does in no way suggest that you ignore or deny problems. It simply means that you are aware that no problem has power over you.
- There are different levels of confidence.
- Confidence levels are fluid, meaning they are sometimes high and sometimes low depending on the situation.

Essential Questions

- What is confidence? How can you demonstrate confidence?
- How will you describe and differentiate levels of confidence? Give specific examples.
- What did you learn about confidence in this chapter?
- How might you apply what you learned to increase your confidence in these four areas of your life: health, education, career, and relationships?

College and Career Readiness Anchor Standards

- Reading Standards: R.CCR. 1, 2, 3, 4, 7, 8, 9, and 10.
- Writing Standards: W.CCR. 1, 2, 3, 4, 5, 6, 7, 8, 9, and 10.
- Speaking and Listening Standards:SL.CCR.1, 2, 3, 4, 5, and 6.
- Language Standards: L.CCR.1, 2, 3, 4, 5 and 6.

S ELF-CONFIDENCE IS YET another benefit of transformation that you've gained because of undertaking this journey toward your *pull to become.* Your *pull to become* is constantly tugging at your heart. You recognized it through your desires and dissatisfaction. You wrote it down and you read it aloud to yourself every day. Every time you thought about this *pull to become*, you came alive, your heart skipped a beat, and you were excited. Thinking about your *pull to become* still excites you now because you know it is good for you and that it will benefit others as well. It aligns with your core values, and you feel at peace with it!

When you took the leap out of your comfort zone and into the unfamiliar territory of the *pull*, you made one of the most courageous moves of your life. Since then, you have never looked back. It's been a long journey with many twists and turns, many surprises, and many obstacles. Fear and self-doubt have been a constant companion, but you also have empowering tools in your arsenal to face fear and edge it to the corner of your mind. In so doing, you have tamed fear and self-doubt, ensuring that they no longer have the power to control your life and influence your decisions. You have evolved. Now you are filled with faith, and you are confident! You may be knocked down, but never knocked out! With every fall, you exercise your capacity to rise up, dust off, and advance confidently toward your *pull to become.* You no longer ignore your "gut" feelings. Rather, you recognize and honor these as your natural guidance and protection system (G.P.S.), especially when you hit a roadblock. You use your intuitive capacity to generate new ideas and initiate new action plans. You follow your *pull to become* rather than follow the crowd. You chart your own course to a brighter future, and you lead but do not hesitate to reach out for help as needed. You forge ahead confidently, knowing that there is a pathway even if it is not immediately visible to you. You realize that there is no question without an answer and no problem without a solution; you know that life is on your side. Your confidence has increased along this journey. You are now self-assured and self-reliant. You live your life with passion and audacity!

On this journey, you have also had the opportunity to become more and more aware of who you really are and your place in this world. You are aware that you are deserving of all the good that life has to offer, and you assertively make this claim by virtue of your birthright. You know that circumstances, situations, history and problems do not have to dictate your future without your agreement. You really do have the power to choose how you will respond to any circumstance and the meaning you will attribute to any difficult situation or setback in your experience. You understand that you are the director of your own thinking and that everything in life, including your experience of it, is hardly rigid but forever plastic to your own thinking. You are cognizant of the truth that whatever you claim in your thoughts, you claim in your experience. This awareness breeds confidence because it means you can claim any experience you want by simply claiming it in your thoughts. You have become a bold thinker because you took this journey.

And yes, believe it or not, you have gone through different phases of confidence on this expedition. The first was the *"poor-me"* phase. This was the phase that feels as if life is happening to you and you are powerless. In this phase, your conversations typically center around statements like, *"Why did this happen to me?" "Look at what my parents did to me." "Look at what people (teacher, professor, best friend, boyfriend, girlfriend, sister, brother, uncle, family, etc.) did to me." "Look at what my boss, co-worker is doing to me." "Look at this and look at that … and it's always happening to me."* Take heart and know that you are not alone. Somehow, we have all been there, even the most confident of us. It is self-pity in disguise. In this phase, you feel like a victim and you are constantly telling stories of victimhood to anyone who will listen. This is a very powerless way to live; there is no energy available in this phase for achieving your *pull to become.* You are struggling just to survive. It is the no- confidence zone.

In the process of yielding to your *pull to become,* you have quickly learned to move past this state of perceived victimhood. You have risen above the naming, blaming, shaming, and gaming mode of operation. You have let go of "victim thinking," have accepted responsibility (response ability), and evolved into the *"in-me"* phase—the first level of confidence. In this phase, you are convinced that the world is a friendly place after all, and that life is for you and not against you. You are certain that the power of good in this world has an idea for your life that is better than mere survival. Within you is something more wonderful, magnificent, and fulfilling— something that wants to make a difference on this planet. Now you are able to state, *"I have the response-ability to choose how I react to something. I have the power in me to choose the meaning I attribute to every experience. I have the wisdom in me to choose to become better and not bitter over what happens. I have the strength in me to choose whether to feel defeated or to turn failure into favor."* At this stage, you are sure that life really is not happening to you, but rather, that life is happening in you. You have the ability to choose how you will respond to whatever life throws your way. You choose your experiences. You are no longer reactive. Instead, you are responsive because you are aware of the power within to choose. At this *in-me* phase, your confidence is budding.

Then, you grew into the third phase, the *"with and through-me"* phase. At this phase, you are aware that life is seeking to become more of itself through you. Life wants to use you as a channel through which to deliver good to humanity. You know this from your *pull to become* and your *purpose for learning.* And in this *with and through-me* phase, you are open and available to life. You listen for inner guidance and receptive to ideas, information, support, etc. Your pull and purpose are in alignment and you are confident that life is working with you to create success that extends beyond you to bless others as well. So you move confidently toward your *pull to become* and then focus your energy into the realization of this *pull.* This means you work diligently, you seek and get support, you honor your gut feelings, and you do everything you know how to do—all with a belief in the power of good. In addition, you give up some control (the my-way or my-timing thinking), and surrender to divine guidance. You are confident that unlimited opportunities are available to you and that the possibilities for your future are limited only by your own thinking. You know that life will show up for you any way you choose. As an active and powerful co-creator with life, you cooperate and work with the natural/ physical laws of life. You begin to understand that it is possible to create deliberately. And in this state, you are confident in your ability to achieve your *pull to become*.

There exists yet a higher level of confidence. It is the *"as-me"* phase. In this phase, you've come to recognize that *if it's going to be, it's up to me*. You are acutely aware that you breathe in the same air as do those whom you most admire. The same life energy that moves Oprah Winfrey, Bill Gates, Michael Jordan, and other successful people you know, also moves you. In fact, you realize that this life energy is present everywhere and that you can create anything you want because the life in you is creative. You and I get to decide how much we will allow that life energy to move and express in, through and as us. It's like going to the ocean with a spoon, bucket or barrel. You can only get as much water as your container can hold. And if you decide you do not want to be limited by a container, you understand that it is possible for you to swim in this ocean and enjoy as much water as you want, for as long as you want. So it is, in the *as-me* phase. You take initiative and are self-directed. You instinctively know what to do, when to do it, and how to go about it. You have become deeply rooted in the truth that everything is possible for you. You consistently remind yourself that there is no separation, no real gap between you and your desires. And whenever you come up against obstacles, you say to that obstacle, *"Be moved,"* and you will rest assured that either the obstacle will be removed or you will rise up above it to a place of better understanding and clarity.

Even so, there will still be challenges in your life – betrayals, loss of reputation, ill health, etc. Difficulties will occur. However, you will be able to say with certainty that they have no power over you.

This in no way suggests that you will ignore or deny the challenges; you will simply be denying its power to control your future and stop you from achieving your *pull to become.* Eleanor Roosevelt said it clearly in this statement: *"All the water in the world cannot drown you unless it gets inside of you."* You get to choose what gets inside of you, what controls your mind, what controls your emotions, and which thinking dominates your day. At this phase, you are operating with super confidence!

Now, be aware that your confidence levels are fluid, meaning that it is possible to move from the powerful and super confident *as-me* phase to the powerless victimhood *poor-me* phase. You could fluctuate anywhere in between these phases, depending on where you focus your thoughts and what meaning you give to the experiences of your life. For example, holding resentment can take you right back to the *poor-me* phase just as easily as forgiveness can catapult you to the higher phases. So, when challenges show up in your life, simply refuse to be a victim. Look beyond the situation with the confidence that life is on your side and it will soon reveal the way forward because you are *No Less than Genius!*

As a genius, you radiate confidence in every aspect of your life: health, education, career, and relationships. You groom yourself well – looking clean and fresh at all times. You work hard in school because you understand your *purpose for learning.* In all situations, especially at work, you play to your strengths. This means you focus on doing the things you are best at. You know not to worry about any imperfections. With practice, you understand that you can improve and minimize your shortcomings. In your relationships, you practice giving and receiving compliments. You smile, look people in the eye, and give firm handshakes or warm embraces. You feel good in your own skin even when others disapprove of you and what you are about. Stay the course, and your confidence level will grow with every step you take on this journey of discovery, empowerment, and transformation.

CHAPTER 12

SELF-MASTERY

As soon as you trust yourself, you will know how to live.
—Johann Wolfgang von Goethe

Objectives

- Learners will be able to write a paragraph to demonstrate their understanding of the concept of self-mastery.
- Learners will be able to create and maintain a daily behavior and time-management log.
- Learners will be able to speak to why they created a behavior and time-management log, and how they evaluate their level of self-mastery.
- Learners will be able to write a paragraph summarizing what they have learned about self-mastery in this chapter.
- Learners will be able to apply what they have learned to help a friend manage their time and monitor self-sabotaging behaviors.

Enduring Understandings

- Growth and transformation are continuous evolutionary processes.
- Self-mastery comes with continuous practice.
- Amongst other things, self-mastery means you are no longer reactive but instead, responsive.

- Trusting your inner guidance, aka gut feeling, is an important aspect of self-mastery.

Essential Questions

- What is self-mastery?
- How do you know you are mastering yourself? (Give evidence from behavior log entries.)
- What did you learn from this chapter about self-mastery?
- How might you apply what you have learned to help a friend manage their time and monitor self-sabotaging behaviors?

College and Career Readiness Anchor Standards

- Reading Standards: R.CCR. 1, 2, 3, 4, 7, 8, 9, and 10.
- Writing Standards: W.CCR. 1, 2, 3, 4, 5, 6, 7, 8, 9, and 10.
- Speaking and Listening Standards: SL.CCR.1, 2, 3, 4, 5, and 6.
- Language Standards: L.CCR.1, 2, 3, 4, 5 and 6.

WELCOME TO THE final chapter of this course. Self-mastery sounds like the ultimate, a completion, but it is also a new beginning. How is that? It is because growth and transformation are part of a continuous process of evolution—an ever-expanding upward *pull to become* more. There is no limit to the good that's possible for you. Who you have become - your personal transformation because of taking this journey enables you to embark on and achieve bigger and bigger dreams over time. That is self-mastery! You have become the master of your life, the captain of your ship and you can steer your life in any direction you choose. Better yet, you know you can create anything you want. As a self-realized captain, it is no longer possible for you to look at yourself without wonder. Whenever you reflect on how far you have come, you are amazed by every accomplishment. Undoubtedly, you have learned to master many aspects of your life: health, education, career, and relationships. You have gained a heightened intuitive capacity; you are always in touch, and you pay attention to that still, small voice, or your gut feeling – that unconscious knowing that nudges you to do something without telling you why or how. You realize this voice come from an inner place - your genius mind.

You've learned to value this inner guidance and protection system (G.P.S.) when you are at a crossroad and don't know how to proceed. Having mastered yourself, you have learned how your G.P.S. speaks to you—as an inner small voice, a hunch, a distinctive body sensation, etc. You are wise to open up to it, listen to it, value it, and act on it! The more you acknowledge its presence, the more easily you recognize its guidance and protective signals. As a result, you make the right moves at the right time and place. You attract the right people, engage in uplifting conversations, make better decisions, choices, etc. You become wiser and more self-assured because you trust that your inner G.P.S. knows—even if you don't.

We all may be able to recall times when we have known something subconsciously. Maybe you are heading out in the morning to meet with a member of your support team. You hear or you think, *take the street.* Immediately your ordinary reasoning mind asks, *"Take the street? Why? I usually take the freeway; it's the fastest route. Besides, traffic is typically light on the freeway at this time of the day. Moreover, it is the most direct route to my destination. You know what? I am not taking the street—it doesn't make sense!"* You use your reasoning mind to argue with this insight and you ignore the guidance that your G.P.S. is offering you. So you take the freeway. Ten minutes after entering the freeway, you run into a traffic jam. It is bumper-to-bumper. You turn on the radio for traffic news and you hear this: *a car broke down on the freeway, and another car just ran into the disabled vehicle causing a mile-long traffic buildup.* You are locked in; there is no exit nearby. By a conservative estimate, you are going to be at least an hour late for your appointment. Then you say to yourself, *"Damn it—I knew it! Something told me to take the street, but I just did not listen. Instead, I argued."* That "something" is your intuition, your inner G.P.S.

Honoring your G.P.S. is an important part of self-mastery. Because the essence of this internal G.P.S. cannot be captured by descriptive words, you may have heard some people simply refer to it as a "sixth sense." Your journey thus far has taught you the value of recognizing and responding to this sixth sense. When it shows up as a still small voice, you have learned how to distinguish this voice from the distractions of mind chatter, collective human beliefs, history, stories, messages from the media and other people, etc. You have learned to read the dial of your inner G.P.S. that will provide the answers you need for the next steps you must take toward realizing your *pull to become.* By undertaking this journey, you have also learned to strengthen your resolve, paying close attention to your *pull to become.* The more you focus on your *pull to become,* the more your internal G.P.S. will provide information about how to achieve it. Sometimes this information may come as a deluge or as a flash of inspiration. It may be very clear and direct, or fuzzy and convoluted. Either way, I encourage you to listen and learn, tune inwards, and to be curious. Try to understand the unique way through which your inner G.P.S. speaks to you. You are aware that there is wisdom in this voice. On many occasions, it has meant the difference between my experience of success or lack thereof. Know that the better you recognize your inner G.P.S., the better you understand and master yourself.

In mastering yourself, you've also realized the value of taking time to be alone. This has helped you relax and reflect. You have included downtimes in your action plan to take care of your physical health and social-emotional wellbeing. You manage your time wisely. You are most often engaged in productive activities – staying true to your *purpose for learning*, studying, honing your job skills and talents. You are also more mindful than ever before. This means that you notice your experiences without judging yourself. For instance, if you missed a deadline on your action plan, you simply notice that you missed that deadline and find ways to catch up without beating yourself up for this oversight. This practice has enabled you to tame the incessant mind chatter of regrets, accusations, blame, shame, etc. that typically dominated your thoughts in the past. Because your awareness has increased, you notice everything that matters to you—for example, the way you respond to rude remarks, obstacles, frustrations, etc. You are less reactive and more responsive to whatever is happening around you.

Your relationships are far more enriching and harmonious because of your self-mastery. You are able to tune into your own emotions and spend time both observing and listening to others. This has helped to increase your powers of empathy and your ability to connect easily and in meaningful ways with others. You have also learned to manage your emotions. You consciously choose to release negative emotions, especially feelings of separation and worthlessness, which can stand in the way of achieving your *pull to become*.

Remember, a great *pull to become* is tugging at your heart. Through yielding to this pull you have recognized that you are part of something much bigger. Know that you will create something good on this journey of life. And in the process, you will also gain more self-mastery. That is the ultimate reward of this journey – a life of peace, freedom, success and happiness that comes as with the realization that you are *No less than Genius!*

FINAL THOUGHTS

R EALIZING YOUR *PULL* *to* *become* requires focus, perseverance, and hard work. Over time, these practices will definitely move you forward in the direction of your pull. However, if you would like to accelerate your achievement, it will be necessary for you to unclog your pathway. This means clearing the channel for good to continuously flow into your life. Experts offer numerous daily practices that are effective in removing obstacles to free flow of good. Here are three that have worked wonders for me: *gratitude, forgiveness, and generosity.* Feel free to explore and discover others that resonate with you. I encourage you to incorporate these practices into your daily routine as you advance confidently in the direction of your *pull to become....*

Gratitude is the art of giving thanks for everything: *"the good, the bad, and the ugly."* It is independent of your life circumstances and is a matter of where you choose to place your attention. All things have contributed to make you who you are today, so give thanks in all things, although the good may not be immediately apparent. The more grateful you are for the good that comes your way, the more good will come, and the more quickly it will come. This is so because the mental attitude of gratitude is a magnet that draws your mind closer to the source of good. Without gratitude, it is easy to entertain thoughts of dissatisfaction for longer than necessary.

And if your thoughts are fixed on dissatisfaction—be it with school, work, health, family relationships, poverty, violence, physical or mental imprisonment, etc.—there your creative energies will flow. For this reason, it is necessary to cultivate the habit of being grateful in all things. This does not mean that you are grateful for being abused, neglected, falsely accused, cheated on, betrayed, or enduring some other horrid experiences. But it does mean that you shift your thoughts away from these undesirable experiences which weaken you to the empowering thought of gratitude, which strengthens you. Learn from your experiences, release the hurt, and give thanks for the lessons learned. An experience that you thought was hurtful or frustrating might turn out to be a blessing in disguise—who is to tell?

Many years ago, my five-year-old son was having a tough time with eating his breakfast in time for school. Each morning, it would take him at least thirty minutes to eat a small bowl of oatmeal. He would just sit there and stare at the food until I came to sit with him. Ordinarily, thirty minutes would not seem like a long time, but on a weekday morning, it is a frenzied and significant amount of time in many households with school-age children. I needed to get myself ready for work during his breakfast time. And, since I would not send him to school on an empty stomach, I would drop everything else I was doing and sit with him, to encourage him to eat something. On one occasion, I sat with him for over forty minutes. I started to get frustrated and I let him know. On another occasion, I was so frustrated that I broke down in tears, not knowing how to handle the situation without yelling and upsetting him. I had tried every trick I knew without success. I was often late for work due to this situation, and I hated that. I dreaded school-day mornings, because my heart was always racing and I would leave for work resentful of my circumstance.

Then, one morning at the breakfast table, the thought of gratitude rushed in and flooded my mind. I asked myself, what can I find to be grateful for in this situation right now? Almost immediately, my heart slowed down and softened as I thought of my son. I felt grateful that through him, I was able to experience the untold joy of motherhood. He is my dear son, whose presence in my life added enormous depth to my existence, and meaning to my endeavors. I was grateful that my presence was an incentive for his appetite and that I was able to be there to help him as he struggled with a perceived sense of abandonment—eating alone! This simple shift from thoughts of frustration to thoughts of gratitude changed everything. It was powerful! Thereafter, weekdays were no longer dreadful. I looked forward with gratitude to the one-on-one time that I get to spend with my son before I sent him off to school.

This is an attitude you may seek to adopt. You want to be able to find the good wherever you happen to be, even in the midst of a difficult situation. This will not happen just because you've read about it. In my experience, most of what I know and believe typically flies out the window in the midst of a difficult situation. Only by daily practice have I developed the tools to meet life's challenges in new ways. I encourage you to practice gratitude as this will help you recognize the good in everything—and the good in everything will gravitate toward you.

Another practice for clearing the channel is **forgiveness**. We are all human and have all made mistakes. Therefore, we all carry with us the burden of some form of guilt. We all feel the need not only to be forgiven, but also to forgive, not just others, but also ourselves. Nevertheless, it is impossible for us to experience forgiveness while we condemn others. The message here is that if you quit judging and condemning others, then you will be less judgmental and condemning of yourself. So, condemn and judge no more. Simply, forgive! Let it go!! This will clear the channel to allow the free flow of good into your life.

I have learned that where there is no forgiveness, resentment thrives. Long-held resentments are heavy burdens that weigh us down. The cause or source of resentment may be different for different people. Nevertheless, the effect is the same for all – it can weaken your physical health and overall sense of wellbeing. This, in turn can limit the amount of good that's coming your way. Therefore, in order to increase your ability to attract more good, you just have to let go of resentments through the practice of forgiveness. No doubt, forgiveness is hard work, but it is doable. Like the young man who suffered cruelty in the hands of a misguided teacher, you too can set that weight down and forgive! It is not a one-time deal, you do it repeatedly. Although it doesn't change your past, forgiveness changes your present and transforms your future. As justifiable as it may appear, the truth is that resentment serves no useful purpose for you. It is dead weight that drags you down and robs you of creative energy. For the love of you, simply forgive those who have hurt you, wish them well, and move on with your life. Forgiveness will bring you freedom, peace and happiness.

Practicing **generosity** is the third surefire way to clear the channel leading to your *pull to become*. To be generous means to give freely of your time, talents, money, or other resources to those in need. Understand that you only get to keep what you give away. How so? Because of the law of circulation. If you give love away, more love comes your way. Likewise, if you give away hate, more hate comes your way, etc. If you are generous with your time, talents, or money, these will come back to you generously in unexpected ways! People, places, and things will show up for you in mysterious ways when you need them most. Your good does not necessarily come from the particular people to whom you have been generous. So, shake off the hurt or disappointment that arises when it appears that people did not return your favors or that they treated you unkindly in return for the kindness you showed them.

Life, your very essence is generous. However, many of us experience feelings of lack and limitation. As a result, we walk around believing that there is not enough to go around, and so we grab and hoard. This is not necessary. The sun shines on everyone and never excludes anyone. When you are generous, you open up yourself to receiving ideas, resources, circumstances, and people to support you in your journey toward achieving your *pull to become....*

In closing, I encourage you to clear your channel for good

utilizing the above three practices. Additionally, master your thinking! What you make out of life is a reflection of how you think. If you think you can achieve your dream, the genius within you works jointly with universal intelligence to make it your reality. On the other hand, if you think you cannot, life responds accordingly. So, to create a better and brighter future for yourself, you must cut loose from thoughts like *No, I can't; No, it is impossible; or Okay, tomorrow* and hang on to thoughts of, *Yes, I can; Yes, it is possible;* and *The time is now.* Suspend doubt, trust the process laid out in this book, take appropriate action, and see what happens.

In the 1994 film Forrest Gump, the lead played by Tom Hanks says, *"Mama always said life was like a box of chocolates. You never know what you're gonna get."* In other words, life is an adventure, it is unpredictable, and there is no telling what is going to happen on the journey. However, when you align your thinking and action with the laws of nature, life will work with you to ensure that you actualize the burning desires of your heart. Yes, Forrest Gump may be right about life offering no guarantees, but know this for sure: you have a much better chance of achieving and living the life of your dreams if you deliberately choose from a *box of quality chocolates.*

Choosing deliberately requires clarity of purpose and focus. This means concentrating your energy passionately on achieving what you know you are *pulled to become.* I invite you to keep your attention on the realization of your dreams—and know that it will surely come true! Not always the way you envisioned it, but remember: *this, or something more!* Your detractors have no power over you. Detractors, interruptions, disappointments, and even naysayers will always be there. Simply stay focused, do not quit, hold on, trust the process, practice the lessons learned so far, and celebrate your progress along the way. Yes, life is still unpredictable, but this randomness is sure to work in your favor, because you have chosen to create by deliberate design and not by default. This is how it is done! Try it out! What you become will amaze you as you discover that indeed, you are *No Less than Genius!*

THEORY TO PRACTICE

Recap

YOUR *PULL TO become* has revealed itself to you in many ways but most clearly through your desires and dissatisfactions. You listened and honored both. You decided for this *pull to become a ....* This helped to clarify your purpose for learning. You tested this purpose for learning, and it is perfect for what you are *pulled to become*. You understand that this pull to become would not be tugging at your heart if you weren't able to achieve it. Therefore, you took a leap of faith and moved forward toward it, even in the presence of fear and doubt. You learned how to manage fear. And although fear remains a constant companion, it no longer occupies your thoughts. You've also learned the empowering value of other companions such as productive and affirmative thinking, a support team, organized knowledge, and action plans. Undertaking this journey has transformed you in many ways. You have become much more resilient, open-minded, and confident! You are no longer impulsive or reactive but are now a responsible master of yourself and your destiny. Congratulations!

Suggested Activities

For the past twelve weeks, we have learned some strategies to keep readers engaged, motivated, and committed to their success. Now is the time to put our learning to practice. Please note that the activities in this section are only suggestions. Feel free to utilize only the ones that resonate with you and your unique environment. We are all creative and talented individuals in our roles as learners, educators, parents, or coaches. So, by all means, incorporate your own ideas or simply design your own activities. In your unique way, make each chapter work for you, your student, and your particular home or work environment. This book is a supplementary text, but may also be used as a stand-alone text as necessary. It is especially suitable for interdisciplinary programs that emphasize the critical social-emotional themes necessary for success in school, work, and life itself.

For example, in a college preparation or career exploratory class, the facilitator may dive right into the essential questions posed at the beginning of each chapter. Alternatively, he or she may utilize the question formulation technique (QFT - developed by the Right Questions Institute @ www.rightquestion.org) in appropriate sections of this text to guide learners through explorations of identity; pull to become, the gap, etc. Either way, discoveries from these exploratory activities will help learners articulate a clear and definite purpose for learning. This may be followed by the development of an Individualized Learning Plan(ILP), viable action plans, detailed discussions about potential threats to the action plans, as well as the empowering strategies to overcome obstacles as laid out in this book. By the end of this course, learners will have created a transition portfolio containing all they have learned about themselves, interest, pull to become, purpose for learning, and the tools they need to succeed in college, career, or life itself regardless of their current or past levels of achievement. Wherever they go, this book and their portfolio will serve as handy guides for charting their course to a bigger, brighter, successful and happy life.

Chapter 1: Identity - Who Am I?

1. **Pre-test** *(See Assessment section and customize as necessary.)*

2. **Warm-up Activities**

Facilitator's role	Learner's responsibility
a ▪ Introduce and guide brainstorming activity. ▪ Write the words on the board.	▪ Brainstorm words commonly associated with *identity*, such as gender, race, religion, ability, etc.
b. ▪ Model the use of a graphic organizer (e.g., Frayer Model) for vocabulary development.	▪ Utilize the Frayer Model to define unfamiliar words.
c. ▪ Show a movie or other media forms about identity (YouTube, TJOP and TEDx are great sources).	▪ Watch movie and take copious notes about actions or words that relate to *"identity."*

3. **Main Activity**

Facilitator's role	Learner's responsibility
a ▪ Introduce the QFT rules for producing questions (see Resource section - courtesy of RQI@ www.rightquestions.org) ▪ Facilitate discussions about the challenges identified by learners.	▪ Think about and name possible challenges to the rules. Write down the challenges. ▪ Document possible solutions.
b ▪ Write or display a Question Focus (QF) related to *identity* on the board.	▪ Generate your own questions about the QF using the QFT rules.

c	• Introduce the concept of closed- or open-ended questions. • Guide learners as they prioritize their questions.	• Improve your questions by categorizing them as either closed- or open-ended. • Prioritize your questions and justify order of priority.
d	• Facilitate a round-robin read-aloud of chapter 1. • Facilitate small group discussion about the content of chapter 1.	• Actively participate in the reading activity. • Actively participate in the small group discussion activity.
e	• Facilitate discussions about next steps i.e. how to use the questions generated.	• Decide on how you will use your questions • Conduct additional research, find answers to your own questions and do the following: - Describe your identity using *"I am"* statements - Do a book, movie, or media production for your *identity.* - Summarize what you have learned in this chapter.

4. **Problem Solving and Knowledge Application for Learners – Journal Entry**

   - How will you apply what you have learned to solving the problem of bullying, isolation or rejection at school or at work?

5. **Post-test** *(See Assessment section and customize as necessary.)*

Chapter 2: The *Pull to Become...*

1. **Pre-test** *(See Assessment section and customize as necessary.)*

2. **Warm-up Activities**

	Facilitator's role	Learner's responsibility
a.	▪ Introduce and guide brainstorming activity ▪ Write the words on the board.	▪ Brainstorm words commonly associated with *pull to become...* such as dream, possibilities, vision, aspiration, desire, longing, goals, aim, etc.
b.	▪ Model the use of a graphic organizer (e.g., Frayer Model) for vocabulary development.	▪ Utilize the Frayer Model to define unfamiliar words.
c.	▪ Show a movie or other media forms about *pull to become...* (YouTube, TJOP and TEDx are great sources).	▪ Watch movie and take copious notes about actions or words that relate to *"pull to become ...."*

3. **Main Activity**

	Facilitator's role	Learner's responsibility
a.	▪ Introduce the QFT rules for producing questions (see Resource section - courtesy of RQI@ www.rightquestions.org) ▪ Facilitate discussions about the challenges identified by learners	▪ Think about and name possible challenges to the rules. Write down the challenges. ▪ Document possible solutions.
b.	▪ Write or display a Question Focus (QF) related to *pull to become...* on the board.	▪ Generate your own questions about the QF, using the QFT rules.

c.	▪ Introduce the concept of closed-or open-ended questions. ▪ Guide learners as they prioritize their questions.	▪ Improve your questions by categorizing them as either closed- or open-ended. ▪ Prioritize your questions and justify order of priority.
d.	▪ Facilitate a round-robin read-aloud of chapter 2. ▪ Facilitate small group discussion about the content of chapter 2.	▪ Actively participate in the reading activity. ▪ Actively participate in the small group discussion.
e.	▪ Facilitate discussions about next steps i.e. how to use the questions generated.	▪ Decide on how you will use your questions. ▪ Conduct additional research, find answers to your own questions and do the following: - Write your vision or *"what"* statement in the four domains of health, education, career, & relationships - Design a vision or *"what"* board for your *pull to become* .... - Summarize what you have learned in this chapter,

4. **Problem Solving and Knowledge Application for Learners – Journal Entry**

- How will you apply what you learned to help a friend discover his/her pull to become, and to convince your friend that it is important to know one's *pull to become*...?

5. **Post-test** *(See Assessment section and customize as necessary.)*

Chapter 3: Purpose for Learning

1. **Pre-test** *(See Assessment section and customize as necessary.)*

2. **Warm-up Activities**

Facilitator's role	Learner's responsibility
a. ▪ Introduce and guide brainstorming activity. ▪ Write the words on the board.	▪ Brainstorm words commonly associated with *purpose for learning* such as intentions, objectives, etc.
b. ▪ Model the use of a graphic organizer (e.g., Frayer Model) for vocabulary development.	▪ Utilize the Frayer Model to define unfamiliar words.
c. ▪ Show a movie or other media forms about *"purpose for learning..."* (YouTube, TJOP, and TEDx are great sources).	▪ Watch movie and take copious notes about actions or words that point to *"purpose for learning..."*

3. **Main Activity**

Facilitator's role	Learner's responsibility
a. ▪ Introduce the QFT rules for producing questions (see Resource section - courtesy of RQI@ www.rightquestions.org) ▪ Facilitate discussions about the challenges identified by learners.	▪ Think about and name possible challenges to the rules. Write down the challenges. ▪ Document possible solutions.
b. ▪ Write or display a Question Focus (QF) about *purpose for learning* on the board.	▪ Generate your own questions about the QF using the QFT rules.

c.	▪ Introduce the concept of closed- or open-ended questions. ▪ Guide learners as they prioritize their own questions.	▪ Improve your questions by categorizing them as either closed- or open-ended ▪ Prioritize your questions and justify order of priority.
d.	▪ Facilitate a round-robin read-aloud of chapter 3. ▪ Facilitate small group discussions about the content of chapter 3.	▪ Actively participate in the reading activity. ▪ Actively participate in the small group discussion activity.
e.	▪ Facilitate discussions about next steps i.e. how to use the questions generated.	▪ Decide on how you will use your questions. ▪ Conduct additional research, find answers to your own questions and do the following: - write a paragraph to articulate the meaning of *purpose for learning.* - write a *purpose for learning* statement, aka my *"why"* statement - summarize what you have learned in this chapter.

4. **Problem Solving and Knowledge Application for Learners - Journal Entry**

   ▪ How might you apply what you have learned to help a friend discover their *purpose for learning?*

5. **Post-test** *(See Assessment section and customize as necessary.)*

Chapter 4: The Gap

1. **Pre-test** *(See Assessment section and customize as necessary.)*

2. **Warm-up Activities**

		Facilitator's role	Learner's responsibility
a.		▪ Introduce and guide brainstorming activity. ▪ Write the words on the board.	▪ Brainstorm words that help describe the *gap*.
b.		▪ Model the use of a graphic organizer (e.g., Frayer Model) for vocabulary development.	▪ Utilize the Frayer Model to define unfamiliar words.
c.		▪ Show a movie or other media forms that illustrate *the gap* (YouTube, TJOP and TEDx are great sources).	▪ Watch movie and take copious notes about actions or words related to the *gap*.

3. **Main Activity**

		Facilitator's role	Learner's Responsibility
a.		▪ Introduce the QFT rules for producing questions (see Resource section - courtesy of RQI@ www.rightquestions.org) ▪ Facilitate discussions about the challenges identified by learners.	▪ Think about and name possible challenges to the rules. Write down the challenges. ▪ Document possible solutions.
b.		▪ Write or display a Question Focus (QF) related to *the gap* on the board.	▪ Generate your own questions about the QF using the QFT rules.

c.	▪ Introduce the concept of closed- or open-ended questions. ▪ Guide learners as they prioritize their own questions.	▪ Improve your questions by categorizing them as either closed- or open-ended. ▪ Prioritize your questions and justify order of priority.	
d.	▪ Facilitate a round-robin read-aloud of chapter 4. ▪ Facilitate a small group discussions about the content of chapter 4.	▪ Actively participate in the reading activity. ▪ Actively participate in the small group discussion activity	
e.	▪ Facilitate discussions about next steps i.e. how to use questions.	▪ Decide on how you will use your questions. ▪ Conduct additional research, find answers to your own questions and do the following: - write a paragraph to explain the meaning of "the gap." - determine *the gap* you observe between your current condition & your *pull to become*, and articulate these gaps using *"I feel challenged by …."* statements ▪ Summarize what you have learned about *the gap*.	

4. **Problem Solving and Knowledge Application for learners - Journal Entry**

   ▪ How will you apply what you have learned to help a friend effectively deal with the challenges of fear?

5. **Post-test** *(See Assessments section and customize as necessary.)*

Chapter 5: Productive and Affirmative Thinking

1. **Pre-test** *(See Assessment section and customize as necessary.)*

2. **Warm-up Activities**

	Facilitator's role	Learner's responsibility
a.	▪ Introduce and guide brainstorming activity. ▪ Write the words on the board.	▪ Brainstorm words commonly associated with Productive and Affirmative Thinking such as positive, optimistic, etc.
b.	▪ Model the use of a graphic organizer (e.g., Frayer Model), for vocabulary development.	▪ Utilize the Frayer Model to define unfamiliar words.
c.	▪ Show a movie or other media forms that *depict Productive and Affirmative Thinking* (YouTube, TJOP and TEDx are great sources).	▪ Watch movie and take copious notes about actions or words related to *Productive and Affirmative Thinking.*

3. **Main Activity**

	Facilitator's role	Learner's Responsibility
a.	▪ Introduce the QFT rules for producing questions (see Resource section - courtesy of RQI@ www.rightquestions.org) ▪ Facilitate discussions about challenges identified by learners.	▪ Think about and name possible challenges to the rules. Write down the challenges. ▪ Document possible solutions.

b.	• Write or display a Question Focus (QF) related to productive and affirmative thinking on the board.	• Generate your own questions about the QF, using QFT rules.
c.	• Introduce the concept of closed-or open-ended questions. • Guide learners as they prioritize their questions.	• Improve your questions by categorizing them as either closed- or open-ended. • Prioritize your questions and justify order of priority.
d.	• Facilitate a round-robin read-aloud of chapter 5. • Facilitate small group discussion about the content of chapter 5.	• Actively participate in the reading activity. • Actively participate in the small group discussions activity.
e.	• Facilitate discussions about next steps i.e. how to use questions.	• Decide on how you will use your questions. • Conduct additional research, find answers to your own questions and do the following: - write a three-paragraph essay to explain Your understanding of productive & affirmative thinking - analyze each of the seven genius-level thinking strategies - summarize what you - learned in this Chapter.

4. **Problem Solving and Knowledge Application for learners– Journal Entry**

   ▪ How will you apply what you have learned to deal with challenging and fearful situations?

5. **Post-test** *(See Assessments section and customize as necessary.)*

Chapter 6: Support Team

1. **Pre-test** *(See Assessment section and customize as necessary.)*

2. **Warm-up Activities**

	Facilitator's role	Learner's responsibilities
a.	▪ Introduce and guide brainstorming activity. ▪ Write words on the board.	▪ Brainstorm words that are related to *Support team.*
b.	▪ Model the use of a graphic organizer (e.g., Frayer Model), for vocabulary development.	▪ Utilize the Frayer Model to define unfamiliar words.
c.	▪ Show a movie or other media forms that depict a support team (YouTube, TJOP, and TEDx are great sources).	▪ Watch movie and take copious notes abut actions or words that relate to *Support Team.*

3. **Main Activity**

	Facilitator's role	Learner's responsibility
a.	▪ Introduce the QFT rules for producing questions (see Resource section - courtesy of RQI@ www.rightquestions.org) ▪ Facilitate discussions about the challenges identified by learners.	▪ Think about and name possible challenges to using the rules. Write down the challenges. ▪ Document possible solutions.
b.	▪ Write or display a Question Focus (QF) about support team on the board.	▪ Generate your own questions about the QF, using the QFT rules.

c.	▪ Introduce the concept of closed- or opened ended question. ▪ Guide learners as they prioritize their questions.	▪ Improve your questions by categorizing them as either closed- or open-ended. ▪ Prioritize your questions and justify the order of priority.
d.	▪ Facilitate a round-robin read-aloud of chapter 6. ▪ Facilitate a small group discussion about the content of chapter 6.	▪ Actively participate in the reading activity. ▪ Actively participate in the small group discussion activity.
e.	▪ Facilitate discussions about next steps i.e. how to use questions.	▪ Decide on how you will use your questions. ▪ Conduct additional research, find answers to your own questions and do the following: - write two paragraphs explaining the meaning & importance of having a *support team* - verbally communicate what you learned about the composition, qualities & agreements made by *support teams* to your elbow partner - create a *support team* for their *pull to become* in the four domains of health, education, career, & relationships. - describe the qualities that each member of your *support team* will contribute, as well as what you are personally willing to give in return

4. **Problem Solving and Knowledge Application for learners - Journal Entry**

   ▪ How will you apply what you have learned in this chapter to help a friend create a support team for his/ her dream?

5. **Post-test** *(See Assessment section and customize as necessary.)*

Chapter 7: Organized Assets

1. **Pre-test** *(See Assessment section and customize as necessary.)*

2. **Warm-up Activities**

	Facilitator's role	Learner's responsibility
a.	■ Introduce and guide brainstorming activity. ■ Write the words on the board.	■ Brainstorm words commonly associated with *Organized Assets* such as arrange, combine, etc.
b	■ Model the use of a graphic organizer (e.g., Frayer Model) for vocabulary development.	■ Utilize the Frayer Model to define unfamiliar words.
c.	■ Show a movie or other media forms about organized assets (YouTube, TJOP, and TEDx are great sources).	■ Watch movie and take copious notes about actions or words related to *"Organized assets."*

3. **Main Activity**

	Facilitator's role	Learner's responsibility
a.	■ Introduce the QFT rules for producing questions (see Resource section - courtesy of RQI@ www.rightquestions.org) ■ Facilitate discussions about challenges identified by Students.	■ Think about and name possible challenges to following the rules. Write down the challenges. ■ Document possible solutions.
b.	■ Write or display a Question Focus (QF) about Organized Assets on the board.	■ Generate your own questions about the QF, using the QFT rules.

c.	▪ Introduce the concept of closed- or open-ended questions. ▪ Guide learners as they prioritize their own questions.	▪ Improve your questions by categorizing them as either closed- or open-ended. ▪ Prioritize your questions and justify order of priority.
d.	▪ Facilitate a round-robin read-aloud of chapter 7. ▪ Facilitate small group discussions about the content of chapter 7.	▪ Actively participate in the reading activity. ▪ Actively participate in the small group discussion activity.
e.	▪ Facilitate discussions about next steps i.e. how to use questions.	▪ Decide on how you will use your questions. ▪ Conduct additional research, find answers to their own questions and do the following: - discuss personal assets and why it is important to organize them - take inventory, list, and organize your assets into two categories: transferable and technical - Summarize the findings from HDT's "experiment with life," as well as its implications for achieving success

4. **Problem Solving and Knowledge Application for learners– Journal Entry**

   ▪ How will you apply what you learned in this chapter to help a friend prepare for a job interview?

5. **Post-test** *(See Assessment section and customize as necessary.)*

Chapter 8: Closing the Gap

1. **Pre-test** *(See Assessment section and customize as necessary.)*

2. **Warm-up Activities**

		Facilitator's role	Learner's responsibility
a.		▪ Introduce & guide brainstorming activity. ▪ Write the words on the board.	▪ Brainstorm words that have similar meaning to *Closing the Gap*
b.		▪ Model the use of a graphic organizer (e.g. Frayer Model) for vocabulary development.	▪ Utilize the Frayer Model to define unfamiliar words.
c.		▪ Show a movie or other media forms that depict *closing the gap* (YouTube, TJOP, and TEDx are great sources).	▪ Watch movie and take copious notes about actions or words related to *"Closing the gap."*

3. **Main Activity**

		Facilitator's role	Learner's responsibility
a.		▪ Introduce the QFT rules for producing questions (see Resource section - courtesy of RQI@ www.rightquestions.org) ▪ Facilitate discussions about challenges identified by learners	▪ Think about and name possible challenges to following the rules. Write down the challenges. ▪ Document possible solutions.
b.		▪ Write or display a Question Focus (QF) about *closing the gap* on the board.	▪ Generate your own questions about the QF, using the (QFT) rules.
c.		▪ Introduce the concept of closed-or open-ended questions. ▪ Guide learners as they prioritize their questions.	▪ Improve your questions by categorizing them as either closed- or open-ended. ▪ Prioritize your questions and justify order of priority.

d.	▪ Facilitate a round-robin read-aloud of chapter 8. ▪ Facilitate small group discussion about the content of chapter 8.	▪ Actively participate in the reading activity. ▪ Actively participate in the small group discussion activity.
e.	▪ Facilitate discussions about next steps i.e. how to use questions.	▪ Decide how you will use your questions. ▪ Conduct additional research, find answers to your own questions and do the following: - write a five-paragraph essay to define an action plan, describe its elements and its importance as well as construct arguments for creating an action plan. - create an action plan and explain how this action plan will help close the gaps between your current conditions and your *pull to become...* - write a paragraph to summarize what you have learned in this chapter

4. **Problem Solving and Knowledge Application for learners- Journal Entry**

   ▪ How will you apply what you learned to help a friend bridge the gap separating them from their dreams?

5. **Post-test** *(See Assessment section and customize as necessary.)*

Chapter 9: Resilience

1. **Pre-test** *(See Assessment section and customize as necessary.)*

2. **Warm-up Activities**

	Facilitator's role	*Learner's responsibility*
a.	▪ Introduce and guide brainstorming activity. ▪ Write the words on the board.	▪ Brainstorm words that help to describe *Resilience*.
b.	▪ Model the use of a graphic organizer (e.g. Frayer Model) for vocabulary.	▪ Utilize the Frayer Model to define unfamiliar words.
c.	▪ Show a movie or other media forms about resilience (YouTube, TJOP and TEDx are great sources).	▪ Watch movie and take copious notes on actions or words that relate to *Resilience*.

3. **Main Activity**

	Facilitator's role	*Learner's responsibility*
a.	▪ Introduce the QFT rules for producing questions (see Resource section - courtesy of RQI@ www.rightquestions.org) ▪ Facilitate discussions about challenges identified by learners.	▪ Think about and name possible challenges to following the rules. Write down he challenges. ▪ Document possible solutions.
b.	▪ Write or display a Question Focus (QF) about resilience on the board.	▪ Generate your own questions about the QF using the QFT rules.

c.	▪ Introduce the concept of closed-or open-ended questions. ▪ Guide learners as they prioritize their own question.	▪ Improve your questions by categorizing them as either closed- or open-ended. ▪ Prioritize your questions and justify order of priority.
d.	▪ Facilitate a round-robin read-aloud of chapter 9. ▪ Facilitate small group discussions about the content of chapter 9.	▪ Actively participate in the reading activity. ▪ Actively participate in the small group discussion activity.
e.	▪ Facilitate discussions about next steps i.e. how to use questions.	▪ Decide on how you will use your questions. ▪ Conduct additional research, find answers to your own questions and do the following: - share an experience of personal resilience orally, or in written form - do a book, movie, or media review evaluating how different characters demonstrated resilience in the face of hardship. - Summarize what you have learned in this chapter about resilience.

4. Problem Solving and Knowledge Application for learners - Journal Entry

- How will you apply what you have learned to help a friend who is about to drop out of school?

5. Post-test *(See Assessment section and customize as necessary.)*

Chapter 10: Open-mindedness

1. **Pre-test** *(See Assessment section and customize as necessary.)*

2. **Warm-up Activities**

	Facilitator's role	Learner's responsibility
a.	▪ Introduce and guide brainstorming activity. ▪ Write the words on the board.	▪ Brainstorm words that help to describe *Open-mindedness.*
b.	▪ Model the use of a graphic organizer (e.g., Frayer Model) for vocabulary development.	▪ Utilize the Frayer Model to define unfamiliar words.
c.	▪ Show a movie or other media forms about pull *Open-mindness* (YouTube, TJOP & TEDx are great sources).	▪ Watch movie and take copious notes about actions or words that relate to *Open-mindedness.*

3. **Main Activity**

	Facilitator's role	Learner's responsibility
a.	▪ Introduce the QFT rules for producing questions (see Resource section - courtesy of RQI@ www.rightquestions.org) ▪ Facilitate discussions about challenges identified by learners.	▪ Think about and name possible challenges to following the rules. Write down the challenges. ▪ Document possible solutions.
b.	▪ Write or display a Question Focus (QF) related to open-mindedness on the board.	▪ Generate your own questions about the QF, using the QFT.

c.	• Introduce the concept of closed- or open-ended questions. • Guide learners as they prioritize their own questions.	• Improve your questions by categorizing them as either closed- or open-ended. • Prioritize your questions and justify order of priority.
d.	• Facilitate a round-robin read-aloud of chapter 10. • Facilitate small group discussions about the content of chapter 10.	• Actively participate in the reading activity. • Actively participate in the small group discussion activity.
f.	• Facilitate discussions about next steps i.e. how to use questions.	• Decide how you will use your own questions. • Conduct additional research, find answers to your own questions and do the following: - demonstrate understanding of the concept of open-mindedness, through oral communication, visual arts, cartoons, prose, drama, essay, etc. - cite evidence of open- or closed mindedness of a character in a given piece of literature - summarize what you have learned about open-mindedness in this chapter.

4. **Problem Solving and Knowledge Application for learners - Journal Entry**

- How might you apply what you have learned to enhance your curiosity and flexibility?

5. **Post-test** *(See Assessment section and customize as necessary.)*

Chapter 11: Confidence

1. **Pre-test** *(See Assessment section and customize as necessary.)*

2. **Warm-up Activities**

	Facilitator's role	Learner's responsibility
a.	▪ Introduce and guide brainstorming activity. ▪ Write the words on the board.	▪ Brainstorm words that help to describe *Confidence*.
b.	▪ Model the use of a graphic organizer (e.g., Frayer Model) for vocabulary development.	▪ Utilize the Frayer Model to define unfamiliar words.
c.	▪ Show a movie or other media forms that depict *confidence* (YouTube, TJOP and TEDx are great sources).	▪ Watch movie and take copious notes about actions or words that relate to *confidence*.

3. **Main Activity**

	Facilitator's role	Learner's responsibility
a.	▪ Introduce the QFT rules for producing questions (see Resource section - courtesy of RQI@ www.rightquestions.org) ▪ Facilitate discussions about challenges identified by learners.	▪ Think about and name possible challenges to following the rules. Write down the challenges. ▪ Document possible solutions.
b.	▪ Write or display a Question Focus (QF) about *confidence* on the board.	▪ Generate your own questions about the QF, using the QFT rules.

c.	▪ Introduce the concept of closed-or open-ended questions. ▪ Guide learners as they prioritize their questions.	▪ Improve your questions by categorizing them as either closed- or open-ended. ▪ Prioritize your questions and justify order of priority.
d.	▪ Facilitate a round-robin read-aloud of chapter11. ▪ Facilitate small group discussions about the content of chapter 11.	▪ Actively participate in the reading activity. ▪ Actively participate in the small group discussion activity.
e.	▪ Facilitate discussions about next steps i.e. how to use the questions generated.	▪ Decide on how you will use your questions. ▪ Conduct additional research, find answers to your own questions and do the following: - write a four-paragraph descriptive essay about the different levels of *confidence*, giving specific examples for each level - summarize what you learned about *confidence* in this chapter

4. **Problem Solving and Knowledge Application for learners– Journal Entry**

- How might you apply what you learned to increase your confidence in the four areas of your life: health, education, career and relationships?

5. **Post-test** *(See Assessment section and customize as necessary.)*

Chapter 12: Self-Mastery

1. **Pre-test** *(See Assessment section and customize as necessary.)*

2. **Warm-up Activities**

Facilitator's role	Learner's responsibility
a ▪ Introduce & guide brainstorming activity. ▪ Write the words on the board.	▪ Brainstorm words that a commonly associated with *self-mastery.*
b ▪ Model the use of a graphic organizer (e.g., Frayer Model) for vocabulary development.	▪ Utilize a Frayer Model to define unfamiliar words.
c ▪ Show a movie or other media forms that depict self-mastery (YouTube, TJOP and TEDx are great sources).	▪ Watch movie and take copious notes about actions or words that relate to *self-mastery.*

3. **Main Activity**

Facilitator's role	Learner's responsibility
a. ▪ Introduce the QFT rules for producing questions (see Resource section - courtesy of RQI@ www.rightquestions.org) ▪ Facilitate discussions about challenges identified by learners.	▪ Think about and name possible challenges to following the rules. Write down the challenges ▪ Document possible solutions.
b. ▪ Write or display a Question Focus (QF) about *self-mastery* on the board.	▪ Generate your own questions about the QF using the QFT rules.

c.	<ul><li>Introduce the concept of closed-or open-ended questions.</li><li>Guide learners as they prioritize their own questions.</li></ul>	<ul><li>Improve your questions by categorizing them as either closed- or open-ended.</li><li>Prioritize your questions and justify order of priority.</li></ul>
d.	<ul><li>Facilitate a round-robin read-aloud of chapter 12.</li><li>Facilitate small group discussion about the content of chapter 12.</li></ul>	<ul><li>Actively participate in the reading activity.</li><li>Actively participate in the small group discussion activity.</li></ul>
e.	<ul><li>Facilitate discussions about next steps i.e. how to use questions.</li></ul>	<ul><li>Decide how you will use your questions.</li><li>Conduct additional research, find answers to your own questions and do the following:</li></ul> - write a paragraph to demonstrate understanding of self-mastery. - create and maintain a daily behavior and time-management log. - summarize what you learned about *self-mastery* in this chapter.

4. **Problem Solving and Knowledge Application for learners– Journal Entry**

   - How will you apply what you have learned to help a friend manage their time and monitor self-sabotaging behaviors?

5. **Post-test** *(See Assessment section and customize as necessary.)*

ASSESSMENTS

Chapter 1: Identity – Who Am I?

Pre-test *(Circle True or False)*

1.	I am my name.	True False
2.	I am my feelings and emotions.	True False
3.	I am the company I keep.	True False
4.	I am my personality.	True False
5.	I am what people say I am.	True False
6.	I am my likes and dislikes.	True False
7.	I am the role I play.	True False
8.	I am my story.	True False
9.	I am my body.	True False
10.	I am my mirror image.	True False

11. This is how I would describe my identity:

_____

_____

_____

_____

_____

_____

_____

_____

_____

_____

_____

_____

_____

_____

_____

_____

Chapter 1: Identity – Who Am I?

Post-test *(Circle True or False)*

1. I am my name.   True False
2. I am my feelings and emotions.   True False
3. I am the company I keep.   True False
4. I am my personality.   True False
5. I am what people say I am.   True False
6. I am my likes and dislikes.   True False
7. I am the role I play.   True False
8. I am my story.   True False
9. I am my body.   True False
10. I am my mirror image.   True False
11. This is how I would describe my identity:

_____

_____

_____

_____

_____

_____

_____

_____

_____

_____

_____

_____

_____

_____

Chapter 2: The Pull to Become

Pre-test *(Circle True or False)*

1. Everyone has an innate pull to become more of themselves.   True False

2. I know my pull to become for my relationships.   True False

3. My pull to become sometimes speaks to me through my desires.   True False

4. I believe I can achieve my pull to become.   True False

5. My pull to become also means my dream.   True False

6. My pull to become is unique to me.   True False

7. My pull to become sometimes speaks to me through my dissatisfaction.   True False

8. I know my pull to become for my education.   True False

9. I know my pull to become for my career.   True False

10. I know my pull to become for my health.   True False

11. This is how I would describe my *pull to become* in the area of my health, education, career and relationships:

_____

_____

_____

_____

_____

_____

_____

_____

_____

_____

_____

Chapter 2: The Pull to Become

Post-test *(Circle True or False)*

1. Everyone has an innate pull to become more of   True   False
   themselves.
2. I know my pull to become for my relationships.   True   False
3. My pull to become sometimes speaks to me   True   False
   through my desires.
4. I believe I can achieve my pull to become.   True   False
5. My pull to become also means my dream.   True   False
6. My pull to become is unique to me.   True   False
7. My pull to become sometimes speaks to me   True   False
   through my dissatisfaction.
8. I know my pull to become for my education.   True   False
9. I know my pull to become for my career.   True   False
10. I know my pull to become for my health.   True   False
11. This is how I would describe my *pull to become* in the area of
    my health, education, career and relationships:

_____

_____

_____

_____

_____

_____

_____

_____

_____

_____

_____

Chapter 3: Purpose for Learning

Pre-test *(Circle True or False)*

1. Everyone has a natural desire to learn and grow.   True False
2. It is important that I know my purpose for learning. True False
3. I know my purpose for learning.   True False
4. My purpose for learning keeps me motivated to   True False
   learn more.
5. I know how to test the validity of my purpose for   True False
   learning.
6. My purpose for learning statement is a living   True False
   document.
7. My purpose for learning is to grow.   True False
8. My purpose for learning keeps me engaged with   True False
   learning.
9. My purpose for learning makes learning relevant   True False
   to me.
10. My purpose for learning needs to line up with my   True False
    pull to become.
11. This is how I would describe my purpose for learning:

_____

_____

_____

_____

_____

_____

_____

_____

_____

Chapter 3: Purpose for Learning

Post-test *(Circle True or False)*

1. Everyone has a natural desire to learn and grow.　　True False
2. It is important that I know my purpose for learning.　True False
3. I know my purpose for learning.　　True False
4. My purpose for learning keeps me motivated to learn more.　　True False
5. I know how to test the validity of my purpose for learning.　　True False
6. My purpose for learning statement is a living document.　　True False
7. My purpose for learning is to grow.　　True False
8. My purpose for learning keeps me engaged with learning.　　True False
9. My purpose for learning makes learning relevant to me.　　True False
10. My purpose for learning needs to line up with my pull to become.　　True False
11. This is how I would describe my purpose for learning:

_____

_____

_____

_____

_____

_____

_____

_____

_____

Chapter 4: The Gap

Pre-test *(Circle True or False)*

1. My gap is the difference between my current condition and my pull to become. True False
2. I know the content of my gap. True False
3. Bridging my gap can be challenging, but imperative. True False
4. Remaining in my "comfort zone" is a good strategy for bridging my gap. True False
5. Procrastination can expand my gap. True False
6. Fear can prevent me from taking action to bridge my gap. True False
7. Fear is a constant occupant of my gap. True False
8. All fears are real. True False
9. It is okay to make fear a friend. True False
10. Making a decision from a place of fear is a good idea. True False
11. This is how I would describe the content of my gap:

_____
_____
_____
_____
_____
_____
_____
_____
_____
_____
_____
_____
_____

Chapter 4: The Gap

Post-test *(Circle True or False)*

1. My gap is the difference between my current   True False
   condition and my pull to become.
2. I know the content of my gap.   True False
3. Bridging my gap can be challenging, but imperative. True False
4. Remaining in my "comfort zone" is a good strategy True False
   for bridging my gap.
5. Procrastination can expand my gap.   True False
6. Fear can prevent me from taking action to bridge   True False
   my gap.
7. Fear is a constant occupant of my gap.   True False
8. All fears are real.   True False
9. It is okay to make fear a friend.   True False
10. Making a decision from a place of fear is a good idea. True False
11. This is how I would describe the content of my gap:

_____

_____

_____

_____

_____

_____

_____

_____

_____

_____

_____

_____

Chapter 5: Productive and Affirmative Thinking

Pre-test *(Circle True or False)*

1.	Thought is energy.	True False
2.	I know what productive thinking means.	True False
3.	I know what affirmative thinking means.	True False
4.	Productive and affirmative thinking can help me achieve my pull to become.	True False
5.	I know the six steps for productive and affirmative thinking.	True False
6.	My predominant thoughts can empower or disempower me.	True False
7.	I am what I think.	True False
8.	Productive and affirming thoughts weaken my muscles.	True False
9.	The thoughts I hold in my mind reproduce their kind in my experiences.	True False
10.	If I master my thinking, I master certain aspects of my life.	True False
11.	This is my understanding of productive and affirmative thinking:	

_____

_____

_____

_____

_____

_____

_____

_____

_____

Chapter 5: Productive and Affirmative Thinking

Post-test *(Circle True or False)*

1.	Thought is energy.	True False
2.	I know what productive thinking means.	True False
3.	I know what affirmative thinking means.	True False
4.	Productive and affirmative thinking can help me achieve my pull to become.	True False
5.	I know the six steps for productive and affirmative thinking.	True False
6.	My predominant thoughts can empower or disempower me.	True False
7.	I am what I think.	True False
8.	Productive and affirming thoughts weaken my muscles.	True False
9.	The thoughts I hold in my mind reproduce their kind in my experiences.	True False
10.	If I master my thinking, I master certain aspects of my life.	True False
11.	This is my understanding of productive and affirmative thinking:	

_____

_____

_____

_____

_____

_____

_____

_____

_____

Chapter 6: Support Team

Pre-test *(Circle True or False)*

1. Everyone needs a support team except successful people.   True False

2. The people I surround myself with affect my level of success.   True False

3. I can succeed alone.   True False

4. My family is always my best support team.   True False

5. My friends are always my best support team.   True False

6. Creating a strong support team is important to my success.   True False

7. A good support team will always agree with me.   True False

8. The best support I need from my team is money, rather than ideas and information.   True False

9. It is best to seek advice from those who look up to me.   True False

10. Creating and maintaining a close, respectful relationship with my support team will accelerate my success.   True False

11. This is how I would describe my current support team and how I receive and give support:

_____

_____

_____

_____

_____

_____

_____

_____

Chapter 6: Support Team

Post-test *(Circle True or False)*

1. Everyone needs a support team except successful   True False
    people.
2. The people I surround myself with affect my   True False
    level of success.
3. I can succeed alone.   True False
4. My family is always my best support team.   True False
5. My friends are always my best support team.   True False
6. Creating a strong support team is important   True False
    to my success.
7. A good support team will always agree with me.   True False
8. The best support I need from my team is money,   True False
    rather than ideas and information.
9. It is best to seek advice from those who look up to me. True False
10. Creating and maintaining a close, respectful   True False
    relationship with my support team will accelerate
    my success.
11. This is how I would describe my current support team and how
    I receive and give support:

_____

_____

_____

_____

_____

_____

_____

_____

Chapter 7: Organized Assets

Pre-test *(Circle True or False)*

1. I have unique gifts and talents.   True False
2. The sum total of all my gifts and talents makes up   True False
    my personal assets.
3. Organizing my personal assets is disempowering.   True False
4. Henry David Thoreau is a successful American   True False
    businessman.
5. To be successful, I must direct my organized assets   True False
    toward a definite purpose.
6. Self-empowerment means to have power over others. True False
7. Life is creative, I have life, so I am a co-creator with life. True False
8. Daily, I create my experiences either by design or   True False
    by default.
9. I must first decide to succeed, before I can be successful. True False
10. For every minute I spend organizing, I gain more   True False
    time to succeed.
11. This is how I would organize my assets to empower me achieve
    my *pull to become*:

_____

_____

_____

_____

_____

_____

_____

_____

_____

_____

Chapter 7: Organized Assets

Post-test *(Circle True or False)*

1. I have unique gifts and talents.   True False
2. The sum total of all my gifts and talents makes up   True False
    my personal assets.
3. Organizing my personal assets is disempowering.   True False
4. Henry David Thoreau is a successful American   True False
    businessman.
5. To be successful, I must direct my organized assets   True False
    toward a definite purpose.
6. Self-empowerment means to have power over others.   True False
7. Life is creative, I have life, so I am a co-creator with life. True False
8. Daily, I create my experiences either by design or   True False
    by default.
9. I must first decide to succeed, before I can be successful. True False
10. For every minute I spend organizing, I gain more   True False
    time to succeed.
11. This is how I would organize my assets to empower me achieve
    my *pull to become*:

_____

_____

_____

_____

_____

_____

_____

_____

_____

_____

Chapter 8: Closing the gap

Pre-test *(Circle True or False)*

1. I can close my gaps without support.   True False
2. Creating an action plan will help to close my gaps. True False
3. An effective action plan consists of only one   True False
   major step.
4. Action plans are fixed and should never be revised. True False
5. Action plans are seldom necessary for   True False
   achieving success.
6. Action plans help me know what to do, when,   True False
   where, and how.
7. My action plan helps me monitor my progress   True False
   towards my goals.
8. Placing my attention on my goals, and away from   True False
   my doubts is a great way to close my gaps.
9. All action plans are effective plans.   True False
10. People do not plan to fail; they simply fail to plan. True False
11. This is how I plan to close my gaps:

Chapter 8: Closing the gap

Post-test *(Circle True or False)*

1. I can close my gaps without support.   True False
2. Creating an action plan will help to close my gaps. True False
3. An effective action plan consists of only one   True False
   major step.
4. Action plans are fixed and should never be revised. True False
5. Action plans are seldom necessary for   True False
   achieving success.
6. Action plans help me know what to do, when,   True False
   where, and how.
7. My action plan helps me monitor my progress   True False
   towards my goals.
8. Placing my attention on my goals, and away from True False
   my doubts is a great way to close my gaps.
9. All action plans are effective plans.   True False
10. People do not plan to fail; they simply fail to plan. True False
11. This is how I plan to close my gaps:

_____

_____

_____

_____

_____

_____

_____

_____

_____

_____

Chapter 9: Resilience

Pre-test *(Circle True or False)*

1. Resilience means to be silenced repeatedly.   True   False
2. Resilient people are problem-free people.   True   False
3. Resilient people are lucky people.   True   False
4. Resilient people are concerned about working   True   False
   outside their comfort zones.
5. Resilient people do not rely on a support team.   True   False
6. Resilience is the ability to come back after a setback.   True   False
7. Resilient people outlast tough times.   True   False
8. The way I respond to adversity determines how   True   False
   resilient I am.
9. I am immune to disappointments – no need for   True   False
   resilience.
10. Success and failure are not final; it is the courage to   True   False
    continue that matters.
11. This is how I know I am resilient (describe the incident):

_____

_____

_____

_____

_____

_____

_____

_____

_____

_____

_____

Chapter 9: Resilience

Post-test *(Circle True or False)*

1. Resilience means to be silenced repeatedly.   True   False
2. Resilient people are problem-free people.   True   False
3. Resilient people are lucky people.   True   False
4. Resilient people are concerned about working   True   False
   outside their comfort zones.
5. Resilient people do not rely on a support team.   True   False
6. Resilience is the ability to come back after a setback.   True   False
7. Resilient people outlast tough times.   True   False
8. The way I respond to adversity determines how   True   False
   resilient I am.
9. I am immune to disappointments – no need for   True   False
   resilience.
10. Success and failure are not final; it is the courage to   True   False
    continue that matters.
11. This is how I know I am resilient (describe the incident):

_____

_____

_____

_____

_____

_____

_____

_____

_____

_____

_____

Chapter 10: Open-mindedness

Pre-test *(Circle True or False)*

1. To be open-minded means to be receptive to new ideas and information.   True False

2. A non-attachment to a person, place, or thing signals open-mindedness.   True False

3. A beginner's mindset is different from open-mindedness.   True False

4. A curious mind is an open mind.   True False

5. A know-it-all attitude signals open-mindedness.   True False

6. Open-mindedness means recognizing that everything is possible.   True False

7. Growing and learning is one of the many benefits of open-mindedness.   True False

8. Arrogance and open-mindedness do not live on the same block.   True False

9. Open-mindedness means to take opportunities for granted.   True False

10. I am open-minded; therefore, anything goes.   True False

11. I know I am open-minded because (describe an incident):

_____

_____

_____

_____

_____

_____

_____

_____

Chapter 10: Open-mindedness

Post-test *(Circle True or False)*

1. To be open-minded means to be receptive to new ideas and information.   True   False

2. A non-attachment to a person, place, or thing signals open-mindedness.   True   False

3. A beginner's mindset is different from open-mindedness.   True   False

4. A curious mind is an open mind.   True   False

5. A know-it-all attitude signals open-mindedness.   True   False

6. Open-mindedness means recognizing that everything is possible.   True   False

7. Growing and learning is one of the many benefits of open-mindedness.   True   False

8. Arrogance and open-mindedness do not live on the same block.   True   False

9. Open-mindedness means to take opportunities for granted.   True   False

10. I am open-minded; therefore, anything goes.   True   False

11. I know I am open-minded because (describe an incident):

_____

_____

_____

_____

_____

_____

_____

_____

_____

_____

Chapter 11: Confidence

Pre-test *(Circle True or False)*

1. Confidence is a benefit of transformation.   True False
2. Confidence means knowing that the world is for   True False
   me and not against me.
3. Confidence means everything is possible for   True False
   others, but not for me.
4. Confident people simply have no problems.   True False
5. Confidence means I am entitled to everything.   True False
6. Telling stories of victimhood is a sign of confidence.   True False
7. Confidence levels can change depending on   True False
   the situation.
8. The awareness that no problem has power over me   True False
   is a sign of confidence.
9. The more I understand myself, the more confident   True False
   I become.
10. My ability to break free from old disempowering   True False
    habits is a sign of confidence.
11. This is how I would describe my confidence level and ability to
    achieve my pull to become:

_____

_____

_____

_____

_____

_____

_____

_____

Chapter 11: Confidence

Post-test *(Circle True or False)*

1. Confidence is a benefit of transformation.   True False
2. Confidence means knowing that the world is for   True False
   me and not against me.
3. Confidence means everything is possible for   True False
   others, but not for me.
4. Confident people simply have no problems.   True False
5. Confidence means I am entitled to everything.   True False
6. Telling stories of victimhood is a sign of confidence. True False
7. Confidence levels can change depending on   True False
   the situation.
8. The awareness that no problem has power over me   True False
   is a sign of confidence.
9. The more I understand myself, the more confident   True False
   I become.
10. My ability to break free from old disempowering   True False
    habits is a sign of confidence.
11. This is how I would describe my confidence level and ability to
    achieve my pull to become:

_____

_____

_____

_____

_____

_____

_____

_____

Chapter 12: Self-Mastery

Pre-test *(Circle True or False)*

1. Self-mastery comes automatically without practice.   True   False

2. Responding to situations around me is a sign of self-mastery.   True   False

3. Trusting my "gut" feeling is not essential to my self-mastery.   True   False

4. Reacting to situations around me is a sign of self-mastery.   True   False

5. Self-mastery requires that I recognize the value of taking time to be alone.   True   False

6. Noticing things that matter to me is an aspect of my self-mastery.   True   False

7. I am not capable of mastering myself.   True   False

8. Self-mastery increases my power of empathy and ability to connect with others.   True   False

9. The more good I create, the more I gain self-mastery.   True   False

10. Self-mastery means realizing that I can steer my life in any direction I choose.   True   False

11. Here are some instances when I have displayed self-mastery:

_____

_____

_____

_____

_____

_____

_____

Chapter 12: Self-Mastery

Post-test *(Circle True or False)*

1. Self-mastery comes automatically without practice.   True False
2. Responding to situations around me is a sign of self-mastery.   True False
3. Trusting my "gut" feeling is not essential to my self-mastery.   True False
4. Reacting to situations around me is a sign of self-mastery.   True False
5. Self-mastery requires that I recognize the value of taking time to be alone.   True False
6. Noticing things that matter to me is an aspect of my self-mastery.   True False
7. I am not capable of mastering myself.   True False
8. Self-mastery increases my power of empathy and ability to connect with others.   True False
9. The more good I create, the more I gain self-mastery.   True False
10. Self-mastery means realizing that I can steer my life in any direction I choose.   True False
11. Here are some instances when I have displayed self-mastery:

_____

_____

_____

_____

_____

_____

_____

RESOURCES

A. Classroom strategies for Question Formulation Technique (QFT)
http://rightquestion.org/what-we-do/

    1. Ask as many questions as you can.

    2. Do not stop to discuss, judge, or answer any of the questions.

    3. Write down every question exactly as it was stated.

    4. Change any statement into a question.

B. Journaling with teens
http://extension.missouri.edu/p/GH6150

C. Ideas for creating your mission statement, aka your *"What" and "Why,"* or pull to become and purpose for learning statement
http://wvde.state.wv.us/insite/files/Developing%20Your%20Own%20Personal%20Mission%20Statement.pdf

D. Sample career vision statements
https://www.livecareer.com/quintessential/vision-statement-samples

E. Examples of personal vision statements of some popular CEOs
https://www.fastcompany.com/3026791/dialed/personal-mission-statements-of-5-famous-ceos-and-why-you-should-write-one-too

F. Building Resilience
    https://www.gse.harvard.edu/news/uk/15/05/path-resilience

G. Comprehensive Career exploration and planning guide
    www.CaliforniaCareers.info

H. Career Action Plan Worksheet
    www.CaliforniaCareers.info

I. Affirmations http://www.louisehay.com/affirmations/; http://
    www.daily-affirmations.com/

REFERENCES

Anonymous, *A Course in Miracles*. Huntington Station, New York: Foundation for Inner Peace, Coleman Graphics.1975.

Barker, R. C., *The Power of Decisions: A Step-By-Step Program to Overcome Indecision and Live without Failure Forever*. New York, New York: Penguin Group. 2011.

Beckwith, M. B., *Life Visioning: A Transformative Process for Activating Your Unique Gifts and Highest Potential*. Boulder, Colorado: Sounds True. 2012.

Blanchard, K., Olmstead, C., and Lawrence, M., *Trust Works! Four Keys to Building Lasting Relationships*. New York, New York: HarperCollins Publishers. 2013.

Blanchard, K., Bowles, S., *High Five! None of Us Is as Smart as All of Us*. New York, New York: William Morrow and Company. 2001.

Burton, K. D., Lydon, J. E., D'Alessandro, D. U., and Koestner, R., The differential effect of and identified motivation on well-being and performance: Prospective, experimental, and implicit approaches to self-determination theory. *Journal of Personality and Social Psychology* 91, 750–62.

Canfield, J., and Hanen, M.V., *Chicken Soup for the Soul.* Connecticut, Massachusetts: Backlist Publishing. 2012.

Capacchione, L., *The Creative Journal for Teens.* California: Newcastle, 1992.

Charney, D. S., "A Prescription for Resilience: World Expert Helps Explain What Can Make Us Stronger in the Face of Adversity." The Brain & Behavior Research Foundation, *The Quarterly.* 2013.

Christopher, P., Ryan, N., and Ryan, R. M., Autonomy, competence, and relatedness in the classroom: Applying self-determination theory to educational practice. *Theory and Research in Education,* 7(2), 133–144. Retrieved from http://tre.sagepub.com

Deci, E. L., and Ryan, R.M., The "what" and "why" of goal pursuits: Human needs and the self- determination of behavior. *Psychology Inquiry* 11 (2000):227–68.

Deci, E. L., and Ryan, R.M. *Intrinsic Motivation and Self-Determination in Human Behavior.* New York, New York: Plenum. 1985.

Diamond, J., *Behavioral Kinesiology and the autonomic nervous system.* New York, New York: Harper & Row.1979.

Dilts, R., "Strategies of Genius." *Success* No. 39 (1992): October 26–27.

Duckworth, A., *Grit: The Power of Passion and Perseverance.* New York, New York: Simon & Schuster. 2016.

Dweck, C. S., *Mindset: The New Psychology of Success.* New York, New York: Random House. 2006.

Dweck, C. S., and Leggett, E. L., "A social-cognitive approach to motivation and personality." *Psychological Review*, 95, (1988): 256–273.

Dyer, W. W., *Change Your Thoughts—Change Your Life: Living The Wisdom of the Tao*. Carlsbad, California: Hay House. 2007.

Eckhart, T., *The Power of Now: A Guide to Spiritual Enlightenment*. Novato, California: New World Library,2004.

Elliot, A. J., and Dweck, C. S., eds. *Handbook of Competence and Motivation*. New York, New York: Guilford. 2005.

Grant, H., and Dweck, C. S. 2003. "Clarifying achievement goals and their impact." *Journal of Personality and Social Psychology*, 85, 541–553.

Hare, W., *Open-mindedness and Education*. Kingston and Montreal, Canada: McGill- Queen's University Press. 1979.

Hawkins, D. R. *Power vs. Force: The Hidden Determinants of Human Behavior*. Carlsbad, California: Hay House. 2002.

Hill, N., *Think and Grow Rich*. San Diego, California: Aventine.2008.

Hinton, C., "Intrinsically Motivated: How to foster authentic student motivation and build a classroom of engaged, tenacious learners." Retrieved from http://www.gse.harvard.edu/uk/news

Holmes, E., *Living the Science of Mind*. Camarillo, California: DeVorse Inc. 1984.

Kohn, A., "The perils of "Growth Mindset" education: Why we're trying to fix our kids when we should be fixing the system." Retrieved from www.Salon.com

Matte, A., "Kernels of Learning. A new approach to social-emotional skills: Bite-sized strategies and flexible resources." Retrieved from http://w ww.gse.harvard.edu/uk/news

Maxwell, J. C., *How successful People Think: Change your Thinking, Change your Life.* New York, New York: Hachette Book Group, Inc. 2009.

Michalko, M., "A theory about genius." Retrieved from http:// creativethinking.net/a-theory- about-genius/

Morrissey, M. M., *Building Your Field of Dreams.* New York, New York: Bantam. 1997.

Niemiec, C. P., Ryan, R. M. and Brown, K. W., "The role of awareness and autonomy in quieting the ego: A self-determination theory perspective, in H. A. Wayment and J. J. Bauer, eds., *Transcending Self-Interest: Psychological Explorations of the Quiet Ego,* pp.107–15. Washington, DC: APA Books.

Niemiec, C. P., Ryan, R. M. and Deci, E. L., Self-determination theory and the relation of autonomy to self-regulatory process and personality development, in R. H. Hoyle, ed., *Handbook of Personality and Self-regulation.* Maiden, Massachusetts: Blackwell Publishing. 2009.

Pink, D. H., *A Whole New Mind: Why Right-Brainers will Rule The Future.* New York, New York: Penguin Group (USA) Inc. 2006.

Proctor, B., *The ABCs of Success: The Essential Principles from America's Greatest Prosperity Teacher.* New York, New York: Penguin Random House. 2015.

Ritchhart, R., Church, M., and Morrison, K., *Making Thinking Visible: How to Promote Engagement, Understanding, and Independence for All Learners*. San Francisco, California: Jossey-Bass. 2011.

Roth, G., Assor, A., Kanat-Maymon, Y and Kaplan, H., Autonomous motivation for teaching: How self-determined teaching may lead to self-determined learning. *Journal of Educational Psychology* 99 (2007):761–74.

Rothstein, D., and Santana, L., *Make Just One Change: Teach Youth to Ask Their Own Questions*. Cambridge, Massachusetts: Harvard Education Press. 2011.

Ryan, R. M., and Deci, E.L., "Intrinsic and Extrinsic Motivations: Classic definitions and new directions." *Contemporary Educational Psychology* 25(2000b):54–67.

Simonton, D. K., "The surprising nature of scientific genius." *The Scientist*, 3 February 6 (1989e): 9, 11.

Simonton, D. K., Genius and creativity. In H. S. Friedman, ed., Encyclopedia of Mental Health (2nd ed. Oxford, England: Elsevier.), Vol. 2, (2016i): 269–276.

Simonton, D. K., "Intelligence, inheritance, motivation, and expertise." [Review of the book *Grit: The Power of Passion and Perseverance*, A. Duckworth, and Peak: *Secrets from the New Science of Expertise*, A. Ericsson and R. Pool]. *Intelligence*, 58 (2016k): 80.

Schuller, R.H., *Don't Throw Away Tomorrow: Living God's Dream for your Life*. New York, New York: HarperCollins. 2005.

Schuller, R. H., *Power Thoughts*. New York, New York: Harper Collins.1983.

Sultan, A., When Grit Isn't Enough. Education Writers Association. 2015. Retrieved from www.EWA.org

Thoreau, H. D., *Walden*. San Bernardino, California: Black And White Classics. 2014.

Tolle, E., *The Power of Now*. Novato, California: New World Library. 1999.

Tsai, Y., Kunter, M., Ludtke, O., Trautwein, U., and Ryan, R. M., "What makes lessons interesting? The role of situational and individual factors in three school subjects." *Journal of Educational Psychology* 100, (2008):460–72.

Vansteenkiste, M., Simons, J., Lens, W., Sheldon, J. M., & Deci, E. L., "Motivating learning, performance, and persistence: The synergistic effects of intrinsic goal contents and autonomy-supportive contexts." *Journal of Personality and Social Psychology*, 87(2004):246–260.

Vansteenkiste, M., Lens, W., and Deci, E. L., Intrinsic versus extrinsic goal contents in self- determination theory: Another look at the quality of academic motivation. *Educational Psychologist*, 41(2006):19–31.

Walsh, B., *Regulating the Teen Mind: Activities to help teens set goals, stay organized, and keep themselves on track*. Retrieved from http://www.gse.harvard.edu/uk/news

Yeager, D. S., & Bundick, M. J., "The role of purposeful work goals in promoting meaning in life and in schoolwork during adolescence." *Journal of Adolescent Research*, vol. 24(2009): 243–452.

Yeager, D. S., Henderson, M. D., Paunesku, D., Walton, G. M., D'Mello, S., Sputzer, B. J., & Duckworth, A. L., "Boring but important: A self-transcendent purpose for learning fosters academic self-regulation." *Journal of Personality and Social Psychology* vol. 107(4) (2014): 559.

PROFESSIONAL CREDITS

- Backlist, LLC. a unit of Chicken Soup for the Soul Publishing, LLC. for the permission granted to use "Follow Your Dream" by Jack Canfield from the book *Chicken Soup for the Soul* by Jack Canfield and Mark Victor Hansen. Copyright 2012 by Chicken Soup for the Soul Publishing, LLC.
- Harvard Education Publishing Group, Cambridge Massachusetts for the permission granted to use the "Question Formulation Technique" by Dan Rothstein and Luz Santana from the book *Make Just One Change.* Copyright 2011.
- Mary Morrissey of Life Mastery Institute for permission granted to use adaptations to the following stories:

  - Pregnant tiger,
  - Two teenagers and the village Wiseman,
  - Wealthy & highly educated man seeking the secret of life.

- New World Library, Novato California for the permission granted to use excerpts from the book *The Power of Now.* Copyright 2004 by Eckhart Tolle.

ACKNOWLEDGMENTS

FIRST AND FOREMOST, my deepest gratitude goes to my beloved husband and best friend, Timothy, for the self-less love and unwavering support that made this book possible. Thank you for always standing with me and for me! To our two sons, TeeJay and Etan, and our grandchildren, Jayah and Jahsiah: Simply knowing that you are all doing well empowers me to be and do more. I appreciate your independent spirits. And to other members of my support team, Maxwell Meju and Fola Adisa, I am eternally grateful for your words of encouragement, review of the manuscript, and practical insights. Without you, the manuscript might not have been completed. Many thanks for believing in me.

My profound gratitude also goes to my professional mentors and friends. Perry Wiseman, many thanks for writing the foreword to this book, even at a moment's notice. Your generosity of time, support, kindness, and expert counsel means the world to me. Mary Morrissey, I am forever indebted to you for your mentorship, authenticity, and endorsement. Your sharing of inspiring personal stories and experiences laid the foundation for this work. Michael Bernard Beckwith, it is gratifying to have you as my spiritual teacher and partner in believing. Your endorsement of this book is deeply affirming. To Harry Obiako and Akuyoe Graham: I am overjoyed by your glowing endorsements.

To my students and colleagues: I remain grateful for all that you have taught me. Sharing your experiences with me, both in and out of the classroom underscored the need for this book.

Finally, to my mother, Doris, and my extended family and friends: I appreciate your unconditional love and support. Life without you would hardly be meaningful.

I love you all.

ABOUT THE AUTHOR

H ELEN E. MOZIA is an educator with the Los Angeles County
Office of Education in Downey, California. She is also
a dream support coach, and founder of Support and Structure
Coaching, LLC – an organization dedicated to helping young
people discover what their heart is *pulling them to become* so that
they can learn with purpose and experience academic, personal, and
career success in accelerated time. In her work, she has applied the
strategies outlined in this book to engage and motivate youth to
stay focused on their dreams, goals, or aspirations. She also partners
with parents in this effort.

Helen received her doctorate degree in educational leadership
from California State University, Fullerton. Her research interests
include school improvement, teacher leadership, student and parent
engagement. Dr. Mozia spends her free time with her family and
friends. She enjoys traveling and reading to learn.